First World War
and Army of Occupation
War Diary
France, Belgium and Germany

40 DIVISION
Divisional Troops
Royal Army Medical Corps
135 Field Ambulance
1 June 1916 - 28 May 1919

WO95/2602/1

Published by

The Naval & Military Press Ltd

Unit 10 Ridgewood Industrial Park,

Uckfield, East Sussex,

TN22 5QE England

Tel: +44 (0) 1825 749494

www.naval-military-press.com

www.nmarchive.com

This diary has been reprinted in facsimile from the original. Any imperfections are inevitably reproduced and the quality may fall short of modern type and cartographic standards.

© **Crown Copyright**
Images reproduced by permission of The National Archives, London, England, 2015.

Contents

Document type	Place/Title	Date From	Date To
Heading	WO95/2602/1		
Heading	40th Division 135th Field Ambulance Jun 1916-1919 May		
Heading	War Diary of 135th Field Ambulance from 1/6/16 to 30/6/16 Volume. I		
War Diary	Bullswater Camp Pirbright	01/06/1916	02/06/1916
War Diary	Southampton	02/06/1916	02/06/1916
War Diary	Havre	03/06/1916	03/06/1916
War Diary	Sanvic	03/06/1916	04/06/1916
War Diary	Lilers	05/06/1916	05/06/1916
War Diary	Norrent Fontes	06/06/1916	11/06/1916
War Diary	Noeux-Les Mines	12/06/1916	15/06/1916
War Diary	Fontes	16/06/1916	17/06/1916
War Diary	Noeux-Les-Mines (Detachment)	18/06/1916	18/06/1916
War Diary	Fontes	19/06/1916	19/06/1916
War Diary	Divion Cite. 18	19/06/1916	30/06/1916
Heading	War Diary of 135th Field Ambulance. From 1st July 1916 to 31st July 1916 (Volume II)		
War Diary	Divion Cite 18	01/07/1916	02/07/1916
War Diary	Divion	03/07/1916	04/07/1916
War Diary	Noeux Les Mines Braquement	04/07/1916	08/07/1916
War Diary	Bracquemont	09/07/1916	14/07/1916
War Diary	Noeux Les Mines	15/07/1916	31/07/1916
Heading	40th Div. 135th Field Ambulance. August 1916		
War Diary	Bracquemont. Noeux Les Mines 36b 1/40000 L25.b.3.4	01/08/1916	14/08/1916
War Diary	Noeux Les Mines 36b 1/40000 L 25b 3.4	15/08/1916	31/08/1916
Heading	40th Div. 135th Field Ambulance. Sept 1916		
War Diary	Noeux Les Mines M.36 1/40000 L25.b.3.4	01/09/1916	30/09/1916
Heading	40th. Div 135th Field Ambulance.		
War Diary	Noeux Les Mines 36B 1/40000 L 25b 3.4	01/10/1916	07/10/1916
War Diary	Noeux Les Mines Map 36B 1/40000 L. 25.b. 3.4	08/10/1916	27/10/1916
War Diary	Bruay Billets J 22.a.55	27/10/1916	28/10/1916
War Diary	Rocourt St Laurent 36b 1/40000 T.9.d. 2.5	28/10/1916	31/10/1916
Heading	40th Div. 135th Field Ambulance Nov. 1916		
War Diary	Rocourt St Laurent 36B 1/40000 T 9.d.2.5	01/11/1916	01/11/1916
War Diary	Sibiville Map 1/100,000 Lens Sheet 3.D 9.6	02/11/1916	03/11/1916
War Diary	Villers L'Hopital 1/100,000 Lens Sheet C.4.	04/11/1916	04/11/1916
War Diary	Lanches Lens Sheet 1/100,000 B.5	05/11/1916	08/11/1916
War Diary	Lanches Map 1/100,000 Lens Sheet B.5	09/11/1916	15/11/1916
War Diary	Mezerolles Map 1/100,000 (Lens) D.4	16/11/1916	17/11/1916
War Diary	Le Souich Map 1/100,000 (Lens) E.4	18/11/1916	18/11/1916
War Diary	Warluzel (Lens 1/100,000)	18/11/1916	21/11/1916
War Diary	Orville Lens 1/100,000 E.5	22/11/1916	22/11/1916
War Diary	Fieffes Lens 1/100,000 C.6	23/11/1916	24/11/1916
War Diary	Goren Flos Lens 1/100000 A.5	25/11/1916	25/11/1916
War Diary	Famechon Lens 1/100,000 A.6	26/11/1916	30/11/1916
Heading	War Diary of 135th Field Ambulance from 1st December 1916 to 31st December Volume VII		
War Diary	Famechon Lens 1/100000 A.6	01/12/1916	12/12/1916
War Diary	Famechon	13/12/1916	13/12/1916

War Diary	Mouflers	14/12/1916	15/12/1916
War Diary	Camp 112 Map Albert 1/40,000 L.2.b	15/12/1916	27/12/1916
War Diary	Camp 17 Suzanne Map Albert 1/40,000 G.8.b8.4	28/12/1916	31/12/1916
Heading	40th. Div. 135th Field Ambulance Jan 1917		
War Diary	Camp 17 Suzanne Albert 1/40,000 G.8.b.8.4	01/01/1917	04/01/1917
War Diary	Headquarters Camp 17 Suzanne Albert 1/40000 G.8b. 8.4	05/01/1917	09/01/1917
War Diary	Headqrs Camp 17 Suzanne Map Albert 1/40,000 G.8.b.8.4	10/01/1917	26/01/1917
War Diary	Corbie Amiens 1/10,000 G-1	27/01/1917	31/01/1917
Heading	40th Div. 135th Field Ambulance Feb. 1917		
War Diary	Corbie (Somme) Map Amiens 1/10,000 G.1	01/02/1917	09/02/1917
War Diary	Camp III	10/02/1917	10/02/1917
War Diary	Camp 112 Map. Albert 1/40,000 L.2.b	11/02/1917	24/02/1917
War Diary	Camp 112	24/02/1917	26/02/1917
War Diary	Camp 125 Sailly Laurette Map Albert 1/4000 J 35b. 6.5	27/02/1917	28/02/1917
Heading	135th F.A. March 1917		
War Diary	Camp 125 Sailly Lorette Map Albert 1/40,000 J.36c.8.4	01/03/1917	31/03/1917
Heading	135th F.A. April 1917		
War Diary	Camp 125 Sailly Laurette Map Albert 1/40,000 J.35 B. 6.5	01/04/1917	30/04/1917
Heading	No. 135. F.a. 140/2161 May 1917		
War Diary	Camp 125 Sailly Laurette Map Albert 1/40,000 J.35 B.6.5	01/05/1917	03/05/1917
War Diary	Maricourt Albert 1/40,000 A.21a 8.8	05/05/1917	06/05/1917
War Diary	XV Corps Hill Station Maricourt Albert 1/40,000 A21.a. 8.8	08/05/1917	26/05/1917
War Diary	XV Corps Hill Station Maricourt Albert 1/40,000 A.21a 8.8	27/05/1917	31/05/1917
Heading	No. 135. F.a. 140/2230 June 1917		
War Diary	III Corps Near Station Maricourt Albert 1/40,000 A. 21a.8.8	01/06/1917	30/06/1917
Heading	No. 135. F.a. 140/2298 July 1917		
War Diary	III Corps Near Station Maricourt Albert 1/40,000 A.21.a 8.8	01/07/1917	08/07/1917
War Diary	III Corps Near Station Maricourt	08/07/1917	10/07/1917
War Diary	Fins Map France Sheet 57.c. V.12.c.8.7	10/07/1917	31/07/1917
Heading	No. 135. F.a. 140/2364 Aug 1917		
War Diary	Fins Map. France 57c 1/V.12.c.8.7	01/08/1917	31/08/1917
Heading	No. 135. F.a. 140/2438 Sept 1917		
War Diary	Fins Map France 57c V.12.c.8.7	01/09/1917	30/09/1917
Heading	135th F.A. 140/2499 Oct. 1917		
War Diary	Fins Map France 57c V.12.c.8.7	01/10/1917	06/10/1917
War Diary	Peronne	06/10/1917	09/10/1917
War Diary	Berneville Lens 1/100,000 I.3	10/10/1917	28/10/1917
War Diary	Grenas Map Lens 1/100.000 F.5	29/10/1917	30/10/1917
War Diary	Grenas Map Lens 1/100,000 F.5	30/10/1917	30/10/1917
War Diary	Grenas Lens 1/100000 F.5	31/10/1917	31/10/1917
Heading	No. 135. F.a. 140/2578 Nov 1917		
War Diary	Grenas Map-Lens 1/100,000 F.5	01/11/1917	16/11/1917
War Diary	Berneville Lens 1/100000 I.3	17/11/1917	17/11/1917
War Diary	Courcelles Le Comte	18/11/1917	18/11/1917
War Diary	Courcelles Le Comte Sheet 57.c. 1/40,000 15.c.5.0	19/11/1916	19/11/1916
War Diary	Le Transloy N 24d. 6.4 57c Sheet 1/40,000	20/11/1916	22/11/1916
War Diary	N.24d.6.4 57.c. 1/40,000	22/11/1916	23/11/1916
War Diary	Trescault	24/11/1916	27/11/1916

War Diary	Blairville Map Lens 11 1/100000 I-4	28/11/1916	30/11/1916
Heading	War Diary of 135 Field Ambulance. 1st Dec 1917 To 31 Dec 1917 (Volume XIX)		
War Diary	Blairville Map Lens II 1/100000 I-4	02/12/1917	02/12/1917
War Diary	Sapignies Sheet 57c H.8.b.3-2	04/12/1917	04/12/1917
War Diary	Sapignies H8.b.3.2 (57.c)	05/12/1917	12/12/1917
War Diary	Sapignies H 8 b 3-2	12/12/1917	13/12/1917
War Diary	Boiry Becquerelle S.12., b.8.0 (51B)	14/12/1917	27/12/1917
War Diary	Behagnies H2.a 5.1 (57c)	28/12/1917	31/12/1917
Heading	No. 135. F.a. 140/2696 Jan. 1918		
War Diary	Behagnies H2.a5.1 (57 C)	01/01/1918	31/01/1918
Heading	No. 135. F.a. 140/2754 Feb 1918		
War Diary	Behagnies H2.a.5.1 (57 C)	01/02/1918	12/02/1918
War Diary	Gouy En Artois (51c)	13/02/1918	28/02/1918
Heading	135th. Field Ambulance 140/2900 Mar. 1918		
War Diary	Gouy-En Artois (51c)	01/03/1918	04/03/1918
War Diary	Bienvillers Lens II 1/100,000 H.4.5	04/03/1918	12/03/1918
War Diary	Hamelincourt (51b 1/40000) S23.c.3.8)	12/03/1918	19/03/1918
War Diary	Hamelincourt Armrgh Camp 51.B 1/40000 S 23 C. 3.8	20/03/1918	22/03/1918
War Diary	Ayette	23/03/1918	25/03/1918
War Diary	Ransart	25/03/1918	25/03/1918
War Diary	Pommier	26/03/1918	26/03/1918
War Diary	Warluzel	27/03/1918	29/03/1918
War Diary	La Thieuloye	29/03/1918	30/03/1918
War Diary	Sailly Sur Le Lys	31/03/1918	31/03/1918
Heading	War Diary of 135th Field Ambulance from April 1st 1918 to April 30th 1918 (Volume XXIII)		
War Diary	Doulieu Map 36 A 25d-4-4	01/04/1918	06/04/1918
War Diary	Doulieu Sheet 36 A25d.4-4	06/04/1918	09/04/1918
War Diary	Doulieu	09/04/1918	09/04/1918
War Diary	Doulieu Sheet 36 A.25.d.4-4	09/04/1918	09/04/1918
War Diary	Doulieu	09/04/1918	10/04/1918
War Diary	Vieux Berquoin	10/04/1918	10/04/1918
War Diary	Strazeele (Hazebrouck Sheet) H.4	10/04/1918	12/04/1918
War Diary	Strazeele	12/04/1918	12/04/1918
War Diary	Hondeghem (Hazebrouck Sheet) G.3	12/04/1918	13/04/1918
War Diary	Zuypteen (Hazebrouck Sheet) F 3	14/04/1918	14/04/1918
War Diary	St Omer D 3	15/04/1918	16/04/1918
War Diary	Longuenesse C 4	17/04/1918	17/04/1918
War Diary	Longuenesse	18/04/1918	21/04/1918
War Diary	Le Poovre (Acquin) Hazebrouck Sheet B 4	22/04/1918	29/04/1918
War Diary	La Poovre	30/04/1918	30/04/1918
War Diary	Senninghem	30/04/1918	30/04/1918
Heading	War Diary of 135 Field Ambulance from may 1/18 to may 31/18 (Volume XXIV)		
War Diary	Seningham	01/05/1918	01/05/1918
War Diary	Hazebrouck Sheet A 4	02/05/1918	04/05/1918
War Diary	Kinderbelch Hazebrouck Sheet 3.D.6.8	04/05/1918	27/05/1918
War Diary	Samette (Lijmres)	28/05/1918	29/05/1918
War Diary	Wirwignes Calais Sheet 4.D. 2.4	29/05/1918	31/05/1918
Heading	War Diary of 135 Field Ambulance from June 1/18 to June 30/18 (Volume 25)		
War Diary	Wirwignes (Calais Sheet) 4.D. 2.4	01/06/1918	23/06/1918
War Diary	Quercamp	24/06/1918	25/06/1918
War Diary	T.22.a.3.4 Sheet 27	26/06/1918	27/06/1918
War Diary	36. A/B 18.c.00 near	28/06/1918	28/06/1918

War Diary	36 A B18. C.0.0 near Blaringhem	30/06/1918	30/06/1918
War Diary	War Diary of 135th Field Ambulance. from July 1/18 to July 31/18 (Volume XXVI)		
War Diary	36 A B.18.c. 0.0 Blaringhem	01/07/1918	31/07/1918
Heading	War Diary of 135 Field Ambulance from Aug 1/18 to Aug 31/18 (Volume XXVII)		
War Diary	36 A B 18 C.O.O. Blaringhem	01/08/1918	23/08/1918
War Diary	ADS D18.a 5.2	23/08/1918	27/08/1918
War Diary	Headquarters U 24.C.2.0 A D S D.18.a.5.2 Sheet 36 A	27/08/1918	27/08/1918
War Diary	Headquarters D 9d. 1.8	28/08/1918	31/08/1918
Heading	War Diary of 135 Field Ambulance from Sept. 1/18 to Sept 30/18 (Volume XXVIII)		
War Diary	Headquarters D. 16.a. 4.9 Sheet 36 A	01/09/1918	04/09/1918
War Diary	Headquarters D. 18.a. 4.9	05/09/1918	07/09/1918
War Diary	Sheet 36 1/40,000 A. 24.d.21	08/09/1918	08/09/1918
War Diary	Sheet 36A 1/40,000 Headquarters E.21.a. 94	08/09/1918	11/09/1918
War Diary	Sheet 36A 1/40,000 E.21.a. 9.4	12/09/1918	22/09/1918
War Diary	Sheet 36A. E. 21.a.9.4	23/09/1918	30/09/1918
Heading	War Diary of 135 Field Ambulance from 1st October 1918 to 31st October 1918 (Volume XXIX)		
War Diary	Sheet 36A E. 21.a.94	01/10/1918	02/10/1918
War Diary	36A/L.5.a.6.0	02/10/1918	05/10/1918
War Diary	36A/L.5.a.60 La Brielle Farm	07/10/1918	12/10/1918
War Diary	36A/L.5.a.6.0	12/10/1918	14/10/1918
War Diary	36/B.9.C.8.1	14/10/1918	18/10/1918
War Diary	36/K2.	18/10/1918	23/10/1918
War Diary	36/K.9	25/10/1918	29/10/1918
War Diary	Roubaix	31/10/1918	31/10/1918
Heading	War Diary of 135th. Field Ambulance from Nov 1/18 to Nov 30/18 (Volume. XXX)		
War Diary	Roubaix	01/11/1918	30/11/1918
Heading	War Diary of 135 Field Ambulance from 1st December, 1918 to 31st December 1918 (Volume 31)		
War Diary	Roubaix	01/12/1918	31/12/1918
Heading	War Diary of 135 Field Ambulance. from 1st January, 1919. to 31st January, 1919 (Volume XXXII)		
War Diary	Roubaix	05/01/1919	31/01/1919
Heading	War Diary of 135 Field Ambulance. February 1st 1919-Feby 28/19 (Volume XXXIII)		
War Diary	Roubaix	04/02/1919	01/03/1919
Heading	War Diary of 135 Field Ambulance March 1/19 to March 31/19 (Volume XXXIV)		
War Diary	Roubaix	04/03/1919	31/03/1919
Heading	War Diary of 135 Field Ambulance from Apl 1/19 to Apl 30/19 (Volume. XXXV)		
War Diary	Roubaix	19/04/1919	25/04/1919
Heading	War Diary of 135 Field Ambulance. from 1.5.19 to 31.5.19 (Volume. XXXVI)		
War Diary	Roubaix	05/05/1919	28/05/1919

WO95/2602/1

40TH DIVISION

135TH FIELD AMBULANCE
JUN 1916 - ~~DEC 1918~~
1919 MAY

CONFIDENTIAL.

War Diary
of
135th Field Ambulance.

From. 1/6/16 to 30/6/16.

VOLUME I

135th Amb
Vol 1
June

COMMITTEE FOR THE
MEDICAL HISTORY OF THE WAR
Date 5 AUG. 1916

R M Hunt Maj. R.A.M.C.
O.C. 135th Field Ambulance

135th Field Ambulance Vol I page 1

Army Form C. 2118.

WAR DIARY
or
INTELLIGENCE SUMMARY
(Erase heading not required.)

Instructions regarding War Diaries and Intelligence Summaries are contained in F.S. Regs., Part II. and the Staff Manual respectively. Title pages will be prepared in manuscript.

Place	Date	Hour	Summary of Events and Information	Remarks and references to Appendices
BULLSWATER CAMP PIRBRIGHT	1916 June 1st	10.30 a.m.	135th Field Ambulance left camp to entrain at FARNBOROUGH, complete with exception of one riding horse	AM+
"	2nd	4.30 p.m.	Entrained & departed from FARNBOROUGH	
SOUTHAMPTON	"	6.20 a.m.	Arrived SOUTHAMPTON DOCKS	
"	"	6.30 p.m.	Embarked 4 officers - ASC personnel & 30 RAMC with all transport on "SS ARCHIMEDES" the remainder of unit on "SS ST TUDNO"	AM+
HAVRE	3rd	2.30 a.m.	Arrived at HAVRE disembarked 7.30 a.m. no casualties	AM+
"	"	10 a.m.	Left depôts by march route for No 2 Camp, SANVIC	
SANVIC	"	5 p.m.	Received entraining orders	AM+
"	4th	10 a.m.	Left Camp marched to GARE DES MARCHANDISES entrained & departed 2.45 p.m. no casualties	AM+
LILERS	5th	10 a.m.	Arrived LILERS disembarked proceeded by march route to billets at NORRENT FONTES	
NORRENT FONTES	"		Ref MAP HAZEBROUCK - SA.E.6. No casualties - Received orders from A.D.M.S. to receive orders of 40th Division	AM+
"	6th		Arrangements made by "C" Section to establish reception hospital for sick personnel	AM+
"	7th		Route march & exercises for personnel - Motor Ambulance Cars joined unit with ASC	M+
"	8th		Nil	M+
"	9th		Following orders received from ADMS - Your unit proceed with A Section of your unit to	

135th Field Ambulance Vol I page 2
Army Form C. 2118.

WAR DIARY
or
INTELLIGENCE SUMMARY
(Erase heading not required.)

Place	Date	Hour	Summary of Events and Information	Remarks and references to Appendices
NOEUX-LES-MINES	1916 June 10th		Msgr 36 B 1/4000 L.19.D. on the 11th inst. The hour of march to be arranged by you. You will report your arrival at Office of A.D.M.S. 1st Division x x x You will take two motor ambulance wagons & your riding horses - no other equipment. You will take one deep ration in forage cart. These unexpended portion, you will not take upon Qr. Master. - The section will probably be divided between two of Cos when you arrive."	JMK
NORRENT FONTES	11th	8.10	G.O.C. 40th Division visited Ambulance - Despatched march to A.D.M.S. 1st Div re orders of A fut -	JMK
"			A Section personnel left FONTES en route for NOEUX-LES-MINES, arrived 16 o'clock, met by officer of D.A.D.M.S. 1st Division - 2 Officers - LIEUT. McNEIGHT & LIEUT WILLIAMS with half personnel of sect. attached to No.1 Field Ambulance - C.O., remainder of section to No.141 F.A. (Weather - severe thunderstorm 3 h.m.)	JMK
NOEUX-LES-MINES	12th	9.0	Officers & ½ detachment with No.1 F.A. proceeded for duty at Advance dressing station at LA BREVE and MAROC north & south - 15 of N.C.O.s & men attached to No.141 F.A. proceeded for duty to advanced dressing station at GRANAY and COLLONNE - the remainder of detachment FONTES. Army Horse H.D. 34 died of Pleurisy 12 - mm - At inauguration of Ambulance	JMK

135th Field Ambulance Vol I page 3

Army Form C. 2118.

WAR DIARY
or
INTELLIGENCE SUMMARY.
(Erase heading not required.)

Place	Date	Hour	Summary of Events and Information	Remarks and references to Appendices
	1916 June			
	13th		at 12.30 at FONTES – Officer charge – No.2. Bearer new hand leg by drinking a tea – whether to A.D.V.S. who had him shot – (Horse found in ambulance with K.R.) Visited advanced dressing stations at GRANAY & COLLONNE	M¾
NEUX-LES MINES	14th		FONTES – M.T. personnel ASC attached for pay – ration & discipline –	M¾
		11 p.m.	Clerks attached on hire (daylight saving)	
	15th		FONTES. LIEUT – FERGUSON – (C section) Temporarily attached to 83rd Sanitary Section LILLERS for duty on relief.	
		3.45 p.m.	Secret order received from ADMS – to effect that an advance party of C section should proceed on 16-6-16 to ALLOUAGNE – to take over from No 36 F.A.	M¾
FONTES	16th	7.30	Advance party under LIEUT MALCOLM – proceeded to ALLOUAGNE 36 B forms D.7.	
"	17	10-15	Orders (secret) received from ADMS (40 D1 1/4) to effect that Unit Ambulance should move from FONTES early on 19th inst to 119th BRIG+DE – area – report at Bde HQrs MARLES-LES MINES for billeting instructions – move to be completed by 12-noon on 19th inst	
		1.30 p.m.	LIEUT – ALLINSON departure to MARLES-LES-MINES – to arrange with billeting officer 119th Bde	
		8.30 p.m.	reported allotment of billets complete area CITE 18. MWp leaving 36 B J 30 t –	M¾

135th Field Ambulance Vol I page 4

WAR DIARY or INTELLIGENCE SUMMARY

Army Form C. 2118.

Place	Date 1916 June	Hour	Summary of Events and Information	Remarks and references to Appendices
EUX-LES-MINES (Detachment)	18th		Casualty report received from O.C. attached dressing station LE BREBIS - No 70549 Pte W. LEATHERBARROW 135-F.A. Gunshot wound thigh (left) sent at duty - report to A.D.M.S. 40th Div	MMW
FONTES	19th	4·50 a.m	B and C Section proceeded by march route to DIVION - CITÉ 18. arrived at billet 9.35 a.m	
DIVION CITÉ 18.		11·35	LIEUT. MALCOLM with party from ALLOUAGNE reported arrived less 1 NCO & 3 men left in charge of stone taken over from 36th F.A.	MMW
"	20th		School taken over for F.A. prepared for reception of patients	
"	21st	6·30	Position with LIEUT DAVIES in command marched to NOEUX-LES-MINES - for attachment to F.A. of 1st Division for instruction	mm
"	22nd	1·30 a.m 3 a.m	A Section with O.C. relieved ambulance from NOEUX-LES-MINES. Conferences at A.D.M.S office (O.C. Ambulance)	
"	23rd	4 p.m	Received orders from A.D.M.S. - to detail M.O. to take over medical charge of 19th R.W.F. - vice Capt R. Pollock name in hospital - LIEUT. W. WILLIAMS detailed, proceeded to MARLES-LES-MINES to join 19 R.W.F. (Weather. Thunder heavy rain)	MMW
"	24th		LIEUT. FERGUSON rejoined unit after temporary duty with 83rd Sanitary Section. Communication received from O.C. B Section to effect that personnel were divided and attached	mm

135th Field Ambulance Vol I Appx 5

Army Form C. 2118.

WAR DIARY
or
INTELLIGENCE SUMMARY
(Erase heading not required.)

Place	Date	Hour	Summary of Events and Information	Remarks and references to Appendices
DIVISION CITIE 16	25th		G 1st & 141st & A.D. and was doing duty at advanced dressing Stations. Heavy draughts from No 21 Sent to Mobile Vety Section - rest. Lunition, off shoulder joint? which took place while driving in Hulluh Crater. 18th Welsh Bn. took over adjoining billets	AMW
"	26th		Received orders from A.D.M.S. to reconn. 3 Officers 3 N.C.O. & 24 men for reinforcement C.C.S.	MM#
"	26th	3 a.m	Y wounded. 2 D.M.S. No 865 - Med arrangements No 23 Active Operation June 7 - Orders received from A.D.M.S. to hold brown ambulances of A Section ready to move at short notice to join A & C brown ambulances of 136 F.A. -	MM#
"	27th		Personnel of ambulance marched to bathe at Mines Bracing. Received notification from O.C. 51st Mobile Vety Section that Black Mare HD. No 36 suffering from "Bruising, paraplegia" - Clement move, Ridor - No 13 (Chronic abseess withers) and Bay Mare Lt.D No 41 - (Paralysis off shoulder) were evacuated to Roan Veterinary Hosp and an Check off annual strength - Nil -	MM#
"	28th			MM#
"	29 -	2 hr.	O.C. No 2 Coy A.S.C. important timesheet of visit — an N.C.O. & three men relieved from duty at ALLOUAGNE by NCO & three men from A'cent proceeding to C Section proceeding to NOEUX-LES-MINES on July 1st	MM#
"	30th			MM#

J.M. Hunt, Maj. R.A.M.C.
OC 135th Field Ambulance

CONFIDENTIAL.

WAR DIARY
- OF -
135th FIELD AMBULANCE.

From 1st July 1916 to 31st July 1916.
(Volume II.)

B N Hunt Lieut Col
R.A.M.C
O.C. 135th Field Ambulance

Army Form C. 2118.

WAR DIARY
or
INTELLIGENCE SUMMARY.
(Erase heading not required.)

135th Field Ambulance

Vol II Page 1

Place	Date 1916	Hour	Summary of Events and Information	Remarks and references to Appendices
DIVION CITÉ 18	July 1st	8 am	"C" Section Lieut J. CRAWFORD in command proceeded to NEUX LES MINES for attachment to 4 An of 1st Division for instruction (LIEUTS MALCOLM & FERGUSON-) Instruction received from OC No 1-7a That No 76063 Pte Bruce PA (B Sect) was evacuated to No 9 CCS (Impetigo)	WWW
"	2nd	3 PM	B Section - arrived from NOEUX-LES-MINES - (LIEUTS DAVIES - ALLINSON & PATTERSON) Under orders from ADMS a medical officer Lieut D PATERSON was detailed and proceeded to take over temporary med charge of 13th Welsh Regt	
"	2nd	3 PM	Secret communication received from ADMS to the effect that 40th Division will take over two new occupied by 1st Divn on night of 4-5th July	
"	"	7.40 PM	Following orders received from ADMS - "Proceed early tomorrow (3rd inst) to NOEUX LES MINES and arrange with OC 141st Field Ambulance as to taking over Advanced & Main Dressing Stations, also ct and handing over your Hospital sick ct at DIVION - Your unit will proceed on the 4th inst to NOEUX LES MINES marching in rear of 120th Inf Bde from BRUAY - Ronti - BARLIN - HERSIN - PETIT SAINS - Your will arrange divnl unit with HQ 120 Inf Bde as to times of march - head your detachment at ALLOUAGNE handing over buildings stores etc to Billet warden -	WWW

Secret

Army Form C. 2118.

Instructions regarding War Diaries and Intelligence Summaries are contained in F.S. Regs., Part II. and the Staff Manual respectively. Title pages will be prepared in manuscript.

WAR DIARY
or
INTELLIGENCE SUMMARY.   Vol II. Nagr. 2
(Erase heading not required.)

Place	Date	Hour	Summary of Events and Information	Remarks and references to Appendices
DIVION	1916 July 3rd	9 am	Proceeded to NOEUX-LES-MINES – Arranged with O.C. 141st F.A. for taking over + handing over.	MM
		12 noon	Went to LES BREBIS to arrange transfer of Officers + men of "C" Section attached for instruction to 127 F.A. and doing duty at advanced dressing stations of their unit to be transferred and take over the dressing station + advanced dressing station of 141 F.A. at Fosse 7 mine + Colonne – Lieut. FERGUSON + eight men to return to main dressing station of 141 F.A. to take over Conv. Btn. before departure of their unit – arrived from DEVION of 135 F.A. on 4th inst. – Returned to DIVION with one N.C.O. + 3 men of 141 F.A.(advanced party) On way back took over Baths at HOUCHON leaving one N.C.O. + one man in charge	MM
DIVION	4th	9 a.m.	Ambulance left DEVION en route for NOEUX LES MINES marching in arr. of 120th Bde. via BRUAY – BARLIN – HERSIN – PETIT SAINS, fort front of march weather very hot + sultry later heavy thunderstorm – noon	
NOEUX LES MINES BRAQUEMONT		4.30 pm	Arrived BRAQUEMONT Mark 36B 9.10.10 L.19.D. at 4.30 pm Took over Hospital Buildings and billets evacuated by 141st Field Ambulance also Patients 1 Officer + seven patients in Mines Hospital + 17 other ranks in main Dressing Station	MM

2353 Wt. W25141/1454 700,000 5/15 L.D. & L. A.D.S.S./Forms/C. 2118.

WAR DIARY

Army Form C. 2118.

Vol II Augt 3

Place	Date	Hour	Summary of Events and Information	Remarks and references to Appendices
VIEUX LES MINES (BRACQUEMONT)	5th		Head Quarters (Main Dressing Station) of Ambulance established – Sick & wounded (from area taken over by 119th B.U. 40th Divn) being admitted – Probably evacuated at Advanced Dressing Station – Admitted Main Dressing Station Sick 10, Wounded 7, Officers 1 – Evacuated – Sick 4, Wounded 4, Officers W. 2. –	AW—
"	6th		LIEUT-FERGUSON W.H. R.A.M.C. 135th F.A. joined on sick leave and attached to Officers Dressing Station (Medical) 137th F.A. – Admitted Sick 6, Officers 1 – Evacuated O.R. 8	AW—
"	7th		Lieut D. PATERSON R.A.M.C. reported sick on completion of temp duty with 17th Welsh Regt. Reinforcement – No 79954 Pte NEVILLE D reported from No 5 Gen Base Depot Rouen. Little activity in line occupied by unit of 119th B.W. – Admitted Sick O.R. 6, Evacuated	AW—
	8th		8 – Col CUTHBERTH WALLACE R.M.S. visited Ambulance (which to B.Os on Surgical experience in War). Army Service Corps personnel horses & transport (less 12 animals – Horsed Carts wagons 2 G.S. 1 limber and 2 water carts) left BRACQUEMONT to their own lines recently acquired by 141st F.A. at LES BOIVRI – Folden Disinfector No 5729 arrived from MERVILLE with 2 ASC steam motor men to remain with Ambulance. Admissions – Sick O.R. 12, Wounded O.R. – 13 . Evacuated O.R. Sick 4, O.R. Wounded 7	AW—

Army Form C. 2118.

WAR DIARY
or
INTELLIGENCE SUMMARY.
(Erase heading not required.)

Vol II Aug. 4

Instructions regarding War Diaries and Intelligence Summaries are contained in F.S. Regs., Part II. and the Staff Manual respectively. Title pages will be prepared in manuscript.

Place	Date	Hour	Summary of Events and Information	Remarks and references to Appendices
BRACQUEMONT	July 9th		Lieut. Henry FERGUSON RAMC reported unit having been discharged from H.Q. 137 F.A. No 26275 Pte F. CORNOCK 18th Welch + No 35453 Pte M MORRIS 18th S.W.B. were evacuated suffering from self-inflicted wounds under arrest	MM
"	10th		Admitted Sick Officer 1, O.R. 10. Wounded 13. — No 28101 Pte MARTIN.G. 18th Welch admitted under arrest suffering from self-inflicted injury. Admitted Sick O.R. 14. Wounded Officer 1. – Evacuated Sick O.R. 7. Wounded 17. – right foot. Admitted Sick O.R. 14. Wounded Officer 2 – other ranks 2 – Evacuated Sick O.R. 6 wounded Officer 2 other ranks 3 –	
"	11th		5·0 Stretchers received from Ordnance Stores — Admitted – Sick O.R. 18 – Wounded Officer 2 – O.R. 2 Evacuated – Sick 6. Wounded O.R.3. Officer 2	MM
	12th		No 75019 Pte Particular E (15?·?·A.) admitted to D.A.D.O.S for employment in Divs Tailors shop Admitted O.R. Sick 5. O.R. Wounded 4. Evacuated O.R. Sick.9. O.R. wounded 4. Inspected Advanced Dressing Station – GRANAY – also Gunshman'' & he went in collecting Station of enemy. – Admitted – Sick Officer 1. O.R. 5 – Wounded O.R. 6 – Evacuated O.R. Sick 2. Wounded 4.	
	13th		Inspected Advanced D.S. at COLLONNE also Regt aid post of Brigade Admission – Sick O.R. 15 – Wounded 1. Evacuated Sick O.R. 5 – Wounded 4. —	MM
	14th			

Army Form C. 2118.

Vol II page 5

WAR DIARY
or
INTELLIGENCE SUMMARY
(Erase heading not required.)

Place	Date	Hour	Summary of Events and Information	Remarks and references to Appendices
NOEUX LES MINES	1916 July 15th	2 pm	Proceeded with A.D.M.S. to inspect Draining Station and advanced Dressing Station at GRENAY & CALONNE - also visited Regtl Aid Posts CALONNE Section. Admission Sick O.R. 15. Wounded O.R. 1 Evacuated Sick O.R. 5 Wounded 1.	
			Under orders from A.D.M.S. - Lieut D. PATERSON proceeded to take over Medical charge of 12th Suffolk Regt from Lieut ROBERTSON R.A.M.C. at LES BRÉBIS as a temporary measure.	AMM
"	16th		No 91,791 Pte GOODWIN J.B. R.A.M.C. 135th F.A. was evacuated to Étaples & No 7 C.C.S. suffering from P.U.O.	
			Orders received from A.D.M.S. to effect that Lieut D. PATERSON would remain in Medical charge of 12th Suffolk Regt and that Lieut W.O. ROBERTSON will join this Unit. Little activity in trenches weather cold but fine - Admission Sick Officer 1. O.R. 8. Wounded O.R. 4 Officer 1 - Evacuated Sick O.R. 1 Wounded O.R. 1.	
"	17th		Capt Revd R. RICE THOMAS C.F. left the ambulance for duty at ÉTAPES under orders from Senior Chaplain yesterday - Admission Sick 8 O.R. Wounded O - Evacuated Sick O.R. 2 - Wounded 1.	AMM

WAR DIARY or INTELLIGENCE SUMMARY

Army Form C. 2118.

Vol II page 6

Places	Date	Hour	Summary of Events and Information	Remarks and references to Appendices
NOEUX LES MINES	1916 July 18th		Nothing important — Weather cold but fine. Admission Sick O.R. 22 including cases for dental treatment at C.C.S. Bethune. Wounded Officer 1. O.R. 3. Evacuated Officer 1. Other ranks 0.	MM
"	19th		Inspection Sir= Berton HOUGHIN — Admitted OR Sick 16 Wounded 1 Evacuated Sick OR 9 Wounded OR 3 — No 643 Pte CALE-F arrived for duty (Reinforcement) RAMC	
"	20th		Lieut W. O. ROBERTSON R.A.M.C joined for duty. Admitted O.R. 18 Sick — 3 wounded Evacuated O.R. Sick 6 wounded 2	
"	21st		No 75107. Pte FURNESS. W.P (135 in + A) wounded to No 1 C.C.S (suffering from Hague regional hernia) Admitted Sick O.R. 11. Wounded 0 — Evacuated Sick Off 1 O.R. 5 — Wounded O.R. 3 — 70cw Low disinfector handed over to O.C 137th F.A proceeded to burn Baton Les Brebis	MM
"	22nd		Admissions, Other ranks — Sick 8 wounded 2 — Evacuated — O.R. Sick 1 —	
"	23rd		Marched to D.S. GRENAY. Admissions — Sick Officer 1. O.R 10 — Evacuated — O.R. Sick 1	
"	24th		Lieut. W. HAIG-FERGUSON RAMC left ambulance to take over duties of Regt M.O.F 20th Middlesex Regt. Lieut W. J. GIBSON joined for duty in relief — Admitted — Other Ranks — Sick 3 Wounded 5 — Evacuated — Sick O.R. 6. Wounded Officer 1. O.R. 1	MM

Secret

Vol II page 7

WAR DIARY
or
INTELLIGENCE SUMMARY
(Erase heading not required.)

Army Form C. 2118.

Place	Date	Hour	Summary of Events and Information	Remarks and references to Appendices
NOEUX LES MINES	1916 July 25th		Admission - Sick O.R. 21. Wounded 4, Wounded O.R. Sick 12. Wounded 2	
	July 26th		Nothing of importance to record - Weather fine & dry - Admission O.R. Sick 16 wounded 5, wounded M.M.	
			O.R. Sick 3. Wounded 4 -	
	27th		Captain W. Williams proceeded to Les Brebis to take over temporary medical charge of 12th South Wales Borderers vice Lieut. D. Viliesid -	
			Admitted O.R. Sick 14 - Wounded Officers 1 - O.R. 3 - evacuated O.R. Sick 8. Wounded 4	
	28th		No 71665 Pte Bristow - F.W. - 135 F.A. evacuated to No 1 C.C.S. for operation	
			(Varicose veins leg) Admitted Sick Officer 1 O.R. 11 Wounded O.R. 1 evacuated O.R. Sick 6 Wounded 2 M.M.	
	29th		Admitted. O.R. Sick 10. Wounded 7 - evacuated Sick 5 Wounded 3 -	
	30th		Nothing of importance to record - Admission Sick O.R. 15 Wounded - Officers 1, O.R. 15 - evacuated Sick O.R. 3 Wounded 11.	
	31st		Nothing to record Weather dry & hot	

A.M. Armit
Lieut Col R.A.M.C.
O.C. 135th Field Ambulance

40th Div.

135th Field Ambulance.

August 1916

WAR DIARY of 135 Field Ambulance Vol II Page 1
INTELLIGENCE SUMMARY

Army Form C. 2118.

Place	Date	Hour	Summary of Events and Information	Remarks and references to Appendices
	August 1916			
RACQUEMONT	1st		Weather hot & dry. Admissions - Officers - Sick 1. O.R. 18. - Wounded O.R. 10. - Evacuated Sick O.R. 11. - Wounded 2	
NOEUX LES MINES	2nd		Captain W. WILLIAMS R.A.M.C. rejoined after completion of temporary duty with 12" S.W.Bs. Admissions O.R. Sick 19. Wounded 3. - Evacuated - Sick - Officer 1. O.R. 5. - Wounded O.R. 5	
6 & 1 40,000 25.6.3.4	3rd		Admissions - Sub-Officer 1. B.R. 11. Wounded Officers 2. O.R. 7. Evacuated - Sick Officer 1. O.R. 2. - Wounded O.R. 6	
"	4th		Nothing to report - Admissions Sick Officer 1. O.R. 10. Wounded O.R. 8. - Evacuated O.R. Sick 9. Wounded 9	
	5th		Admissions . O.R. Sick 8. Wounded 5. Evacuated Sick 4. Wounded 6	
	6th		Captain W. WILLIAMS A.A.M.C. detailed as M.O. to 40th Division Train in relief of Capt. HUTCHISON proceeding on leave. Admissions - Sub-Officers 1. O.R. 13. Wounded - Officer 4. O.R. 16. Evacuated O.R. Sick 6. - Wounded 9.	
	7th		One N.C.O. 15 men proceeded to GRENAY to work at entraining CALONNE SUD Trench for Division carrying parties returning of R.E. Admissions, O.R. Sick 21. - Wounded 1. Evacuated. - Sick Officer 1. O.R. 5. Wounded Officer 1. O.R. 6. Lieut J.D. WALTON R.A.M.C. posted to Ambulance for duty.	

WAR DIARY
of 135 Field Ambulance Vol III page 2
INTELLIGENCE SUMMARY
(Erase heading not required.)

Army Form C. 2118.

Secret

Place	Date	Hour	Summary of Events and Information	Remarks and references to Appendices
NEUX LES MINES (BARAQUE MONT)	1916 Aug 8th			
	9th		Admitted – Sick Officers 1 – O.R. 21 – Wounded – Officers 1 – O.R. 12 – Evacuated – Sick O.R. 9 – Wounded 4	
			Nothing of importance to record. Admission Sick O.R. 16 – Wounded 7 – Evacuated O.R.	
68 / 4000			Sick 2 Wounded O.R. 11 Officers 1	
25. 63.4	10th		Lieut GIBSON RAMC proceded on 14 days leave to England (on renewal of contract)	
			No 28266 Sergt L. PETERS – 19th R.W.F. died from result of G.S.W. in main Dressing Station. Admitted Sick O.R. 10 – Wounded 6 – Evacuated O.R. Sick 5 Wounded 6	
	11th		Admitted O.R. Sick 13 Wounded 6 – Evacuated Sick 2 – Wounded 2	
	12th		A small raid on enemy trenches in CALONNE area was made at midnight – extra ambulance motor cars sent to A.D.S. – first lot of wounded arrived at main dressing Station 2 A.M.	
			Admitted – Sick 19 – Wounded – Officers 4 O.R. 33 Evacuated, Sick Officer 1 O.R. 6 Wounded Officers 1 other ranks 7 – one German Prisoner Wounded admitted & transferred at once to No 1. C.C.S.	
	13th		Admitted – Officers 1 Sick O.R. 11 Wounded – Officers 1 – O.R. 8 – Evacuated Sick O.R. 9 Officers Wounded 4 O.R. 23 –	
	14th		Admitted – Sick O.R. 9 Wounded 7 – Evacuated 7 Sick O.R. Wounded O.R. 7	

Army Form C. 2118.

Secret

WAR DIARY

of 135 Field Ambulance Vol III Augr 3

INTELLIGENCE SUMMARY

(Erase heading not required.)

Instructions regarding War Diaries and Intelligence Summaries are contained in F.S. Regs., Part II. and the Staff Manual respectively. Title pages will be prepared in manuscript.

Place	Date	Hour	Summary of Events and Information	Remarks and references to Appendices
NOEUX LES MINES	19/6 Aug 15		DMS 1st Army inspected Headquarters - Admitted During Station of Ambulance Road between BRACQUEMONT & PETIT SAINS was shelled during day - Body of one man R.7.A brought to ambulance (early casualty)	
16t & 40tt & 25 & 34			Admitted O.R. Sick 51 including 24 own Staffs & dental cases - Wounded 5 - Evacuated O.R. Sick 21 Wounded 3 - taken over from ADMS 16th Division LIEUT. C.D. WATKINS RAMC	
"	16th		attached himself to ADMS 16th Division and is shown on strength of Ambulance Admissions - O.R. Sick 5. Wounded 6 - Evacuated O.R. Sick 6 - Wounded 3 -	
"	17th		taken instructions from A.D.M.S. sent W.R.P. McNEIGHT to take on temporary medium charge of 11th K.O.R.L. Regt — Admitted Sick 20 - Wounded. Officer 1 O.R. 4 - Evacuated Sick Officer 1 O.R. 5. Wounded Officer 1	
	18th		A party of one NCO & 14 men left headquarters to report to O.C. 12th Yorkshire Regt (Rimers) MAROC to work in trenches with C.R.E. — D.M.S. 1st Army visited Ambulance with President R.C.S., medium surgeon - Admitted Sick Officer 1 O.R. 14 Wounded 9 Evacuated Sick O.R. 1 - Wounded 8 -	
	19th		Notching of importance - Weather hot & showery - Admitted Sick O.R. 18 - Wounded Officer 3 - Evacuated Sick O.R. 2. Wounded Officers 2 O.R.6 —	WWG

Army Form C. 2118.

Scrap

WAR DIARY
of 135 Field Ambulance Vol 3 (Aug 4)
INTELLIGENCE SUMMARY
(Erase heading not required.)

Instructions regarding War Diaries and Intelligence Summaries are contained in F. S. Regs., Part II. and the Staff Manual respectively. Title pages will be prepared in manuscript.

Place	Date 1916	Hour	Summary of Events and Information	Remarks and references to Appendices
NOEUX LES MINES 36 b 4 D D 25 - 6.3.4	Aug 26th		Admitted OR Sick 15 Wounded 19 - Evacuated Sick 7 - wounded one - Four wounded stretcher casualties received for Dressing Line - Admitted Sick OR 19 -	
	21st		Wounded Officer 1 OR 5 Evacuated Sick 3 Wounded 14 (OR)	
"	22nd		Admitted Sick Officer 1. OR 28 Wounded 7 including one German Prisoner - Evacuated Sick Officer 2 OR 14 Wounded Officer 1. OR 9	
"	23rd		Following orders received from A.D.M.S. 135th F.A. will take over MAROC Section from 137th F.A. by 6 P.M. today". Admitted Section & details of which to be arranged between O.C. of F.A. concerned -	
		6 p.m	Relief carried out - following addenda to A.D.M.S:- Section orders received "2 Bearers of 7 A Bn 32nd Division will be attached to 40th Division one Section will be attached to 135th F.A. + one Sectn to 137th F.A."	
		6.30 p.m	B Section of 92nd F.A. A/C of Capt LEA reports arrived from BETHUNE. Admission. Sick OR 20 - Wounded Officer 1 OR 2 - Evacuated 9 sick Wounded 6 OR	
	24th		B Sect 92nd F.A. moved over A.D.S. Divisional Baths at MAROC - Personnel of 135 F.A admitted to head quarters - Admission - Sick Officer 1 O.R. 8 - Wounded - Officer 2 OR 6 - Evacuated sick 5 - Wounded Officer 2 O.R. 1	MMS

Army Form C. 2118.

Instructions regarding War Diaries and Intelligence
Summaries are contained in F. S. Regs., Part II.
and the Staff Manual respectively. Title pages
will be prepared in manuscript.

Secret.

WAR DIARY 135 Field Ambulance
of
INTELLIGENCE SUMMARY. Vol 3 — (page 5)

(Erase heading not required.)

Place	Date	Hour	Summary of Events and Information	Remarks and references to Appendices
NOEUX LES MINES	1916 Aug 25th		Admissions (from MAROC & CALONNE Sectors) Sick Officer 2 – O.R. 45 – Evacuated Sick Officer 1. O.R. 8 Wounded O.R. 8	
66 1 40.70 25.6.3.4			Under instructions from A.D.M.S. 1 N.C.O. + 6 men proceed to take over charge as billet warden buildings vacated by 112 F.A. NOEUX + 1 N.C.O. + 3 men to take charge of Ground Baths from 113 F.A. NOEUX	
"	26th		Admissions Officer (Sick) 2 - O.R. 27 – Evacuated Sick O.R. 12. Wounded 7 Wounded Officer 1. O.R. 4	
"	27th		Admissions Sick O.R. 29 – Wounded Officer 3 O.R. 23 – Evacuated Sick Officer 3 O.R. 19 Wounded Officers 1. O.R. 7. (10 civilians brought from headquarters 10 from LES BREBIS & eight from CALONNE were sent to South MAROC as reinforcements to work in conjunction with Regl M.O. + O/C. A.D.S. in anticipation of a raid by battalion in that sector.)	
"	28th	11 AM	Took A.D.M.S + D.A.D.M.S 63 (Rn) Division on A.D.S. + R.A.Ps CALONNE Sector preparing to turning over	
		4 PM	Following orders received from A.D.M.S (40 Divn.) "135 F.A. will hand over the Arrangement during Relations of the CALONNE Sector to a Field Ambulance of 63rd Division on morning of 30th inst	
			Admissions – Sick O.R. 31 – Wounded Officer 1 O.R. 6 Evacuations Sick O.R. Wounded Officer 2 - O.R. 18 –	

WAR DIARY
or 135th Field Ambulance   Vol 3   page 6
INTELLIGENCE SUMMARY

Army Form C. 2118.

Place	Date	Hour	Summary of Events and Information	Remarks and references to Appendices
MOEUX LES MINES	1916 Aug 29th		Admitted Sick 44 O.R. (Two minutes Sentry Court) Wounded - Officers 0. O.R. 5 - Evacuated Sick O.R. 29. Wounded 5.	
36A 40.70	30th		Handed over Advanced Dressing Station CALONNE Section to a section of 3rd Field Ambulance 63rd (RN) Division - Relief completed 1 p.m. Admitted Sick Officers 1 O.R. 19. Wounded 0 - Evacuated Sick 3 - Wounded Officers 1	
"	31st	5 pm	Erri shelling in vicinity of Main Dressing Station - 20 casualties Admissions Sick O.R. 31 Wounded 3 Evacuated Sick 7 - Wounded 1 O.R.	
			B N Wright Lieut Col RAMC O.C 135th Field Ambulance	

140/134

40th Div

135th Field Ambulance

Oct 1916

COMMITTEE FOR THE
MEDICAL HISTORY OF THE WAR
Date 30 OCT. 1916

SECRET

Army Form C. 2118.

WAR DIARY 135th Field Ambulance
or
INTELLIGENCE SUMMARY

Vol IV page 1.

Place	Date	Hour	Summary of Events and Information	Remarks and references to Appendices
NOEUX LES MINES M.36 40000 L25.6.3.4	1916. Sept 1st	1.30 p.m	B Section of 92nd Field Ambulance temporarily attached departed for LES BREBIS to reopen the headquarters of that unit at BETHUNE - (A.D.S. LES BREBIS & MAROC taken over by personnel of 135th F.A.) - LIEUT J.D ROBERTSON RAMC proceeded to England on 14 days leave (on re-inforcement) - Admitted - Sick Officer 1 O.R. 33 Wounded Officer 1 O.R. 4 - Evacuated Sick O.R. 9 Wounded 3	
"	2nd		N.C.O. & men employed in working parties with R.E. at LES BREBIS returned for duty last night - Admitted Sick O.R. 17 - Wounded 9 - Evacuated O.R. sick 9 Wounded 4	
"	3rd		LIEUT W.R.P M°NEIGHT RAMC returned to Ambulance for duty from temp. duty as M.O. to K.O.R.L. Rgt. Admitted Sick O.R.14 Officer 1 Wounded O.R. 9 Evacuated O.R. Sick 7. Wounded 3	
"	4th		Admitted Sick O.R. 15 Wounded 2 Evacuated O.R. Sick 8 Wounded 1	
"	5th		Officer i/c Corp Rest Station now departed by rail to AIRE. Admitted O.R. 38 with (including dental cases) wounded 3. Evacuated Sick O.R.16. Wounded Officer 1 O.R. 3	
"	6th		Admitted Sick Officer 1 O.R. 15 - Wounded O.R. 3 - Evacuated O.R. 11. Admitted O.R. Sick 20 - Wounded 4 - Evacuated O.R. Sick 5.	
"	7th			
"	8th		Admitted Officer Sick 1 O.R. 19 - Wounded O.R. 3. Evacuated Sick O.R. 8 - Wounded 2	

SECRET

WAR DIARY 135th Field Ambulance

INTELLIGENCE SUMMARY.

Army Form C. 2118.

Vol IV page 2

Place	Date	Hour	Summary of Events and Information	Remarks and references to Appendices
NOEUX LES MINES	19/6			
26.B 40000	Sept 9th		Admitted Sick O.R. 24. Wounded 2. Evacuated O.R.Sick 5 Wounded 1	
	10th		Admitted Sick O.R 20 Wounded 1 - Evacuated Officer sick 1. O.R.5 Wounded O.R.1	
25.6.3.4	11th		Admitted Sick O.R 24 Wounded 4 Evacuated Sick O.R.6 Wounded 2.	
"	12th		3 men of H.L.I contact with case of Cerebro Spinal Meningitis admitted for isolation & observation — Admitted sick including dental cases Officer 1 - O.R 37	
			Wounded 0 - Evacuated Sick 1 O.R 18 (including dental cases)	
"	13th		Admitted Sick 17 - O.R Wounded 2 O.R - Evacuated - Sick O.R.10	
"	14th		Conference at A.D.M.S office re troops movements — Admitted Sick O.R. 33 Wounded Officers 1 - O.R.4 Evacuations Sick 12 Wounded O.R.3 - No 19396 Cpl YEARSLEY. W.	
	11½		K.O.R.L Regt died from G.S.W right lung	
"	15"		Admissions Sick O.R. 28 Wounded 2 Evacuated Sick O.R.6 Wounded Officer 1 O.R 2	
"	16"		Under instructions from A.D.M.S - Capt - W.WILLIAMS- RAMC (S.R) reports for duty from down to join 6" Division	
			Admission Sick.O.1 - O.R 27 - Wounded Officer 1. O.R 5 - Evacuated - Sick Officer 1	
			O.R.5 Wounded. 1	

SECRET   WAR DIARY   135ᵗʰ Field Ambulance   Army Form C. 2118.
                         or
              INTELLIGENCE SUMMARY.   Vol IV page 3
              (Erase heading not required.)

Place	Date	Hour	Summary of Events and Information	Remarks and references to Appendices
NOEUX LES MINES	1916			
36-B 4.20.b	2 Am 17ᵗʰ		No 29446 Pte R. NUGENT 14ᵗʰ H.L.I died from wounds of G.S.W. recvd in action	
L2C 6.4			Admitted Sick O.R. 22 Wounded 2 — Evacuated Sick & Wounded Officers 1 O.R. 3	
"	18"		Admitted Sick O.R. 23 Wounded O. Evacuated Sick O.R.5 Wounded O.R.5	
"	19 "		Admitted Sick Officers 1 O.R. 29 (including Dental Cases) Evacuated O.R. Sick 19 W.1	
"	20 "		No 71823 Pte LAWSON H.S. 135 F.A. wounded C.R.3/CCS for dental treatment —	
			Admitted O.R. Sick 13 Wounded 9 — Evacuated Sick O.R 4 Wounded Officers 1 — O.R.4	
	7.30 pm		Name Op Orders No 5 (evnt) received from A.D.M.S (X officer Three 40 Div in Z train on	
			14 Bus Section 137 F.A. will relieve F.A. of 3ʳᵈ Div in 14 Bus Section on Sept 22 = 62	
	8.p.m. x x x)			
"	21"		No 24127 Pte REYNOLDS. A — 12ᵗʰ S.W.Borderers died from Wounds recvd in action	
			Admitted Sick O.R 23 Wounded 2 Evacuated Sick 4 Wounded 4 —	
"	22 "		Admitted Sick 16 O.R Wounded 4 Evacuated Sick O.R.10 Wounded 2	
			26 sick and wounded transferred from N3 F.A. of 9ᵗʰ Div —	
"	23"		Recd instructions from A.D.M.S Capt W.J. GIBSON RAMC now struck off strength of this unit	
			on taking over station of 170 to 40 Inv. Train — Capt W.J.B.ROBERTSON described in	
			Temporary duty as M.O. & 16ᵗʰ Welsh Regt	

SECRET

Army Form C. 2118.

WAR DIARY
or
INTELLIGENCE SUMMARY

135th Field Ambulance

Vol IV page 4

(Erase heading not required.)

Instructions regarding War Diaries and Intelligence Summaries are contained in F.S. Regs., Part II. and the Staff Manual respectively. Title pages will be prepared in manuscript.

Place	Date	Hour	Summary of Events and Information	Remarks and references to Appendices
NOEUX LES MINES	1916 Sept			
36 B.4.D.7.0.	23rd cont		Admitted Sick Officer 1 O.R. 27 Wounded 1. Evacuated Sick Officer 1 - O.R. 2. Wounded O.R. 4.	
25 B 3.4.	24th		Admitted Sick O.R. 19 - Wounded 3. Evacuated Sick O.R. 8. Admitted 1.	
"	25th		Admitted Sick O.R. 16. Wounded Officer 2 O.R. 15. Evacuated - Sick O.R. 11. Wounded 2. No 71863 Pte BROOKE. M F A 135 F.a. proceeded to report to O.C. O Battery R.F.C. in relief of No 30224 Pte WETMAN H E R.A.M.C. who proceeded from unit for duty	
"	26th		2nd Lieut H.S. WINGARD - 12 S.W.B. died (from G.S.W.) in Motor Ambulance wagon en route from A.D.S. Admitted Sick 33 O.R. (including dental cases) Wounded O.R. 2 Evacuated Sick O.R. 15. Wounded Officer 1. O.R. 19.	
"	27th		Admitted Sick O.R. 41 - Wounded Officer 1 / O.R. 2 - Evacuated Sick O.R. 8 Wounded 2	
"	28th		No M/149858 Pte W H MORRIS dispatched by rail to report to O.C. M.T Depôt ROUEN (in accordance with instructions received from ASC Le Base) Admitted - O.R. Sick 27 Wounded 1 - Evacuated Sick O.R. 14 Wounded 2	
"	29th		No 27604 Pte Griffiths H 18th Welch Regt died of G.S Wounds No 71915 Pte INGLEE W R.A.M.C returned to duty from No 1 C.C.S. Admitted Sick Officer 2 O.R. 20 Wounded O.R.5 Evacuation Sick O.R.4 Wounded 3	

SECRET WAR DIARY Army Form C. 2118.
135th Field Ambulance
or
INTELLIGENCE SUMMARY
Vol IV Page 5

(Erase heading not required.)

Place	Date	Hour	Summary of Events and Information	Remarks and references to Appendices
NOEUX LES MINES 36 B 40 25.6.3.4	1916 Sept 30th		Admissions Sick O.R. 24. Wounded Officers 2 O.R. 1 Evacuated Sick O.R. 6	
			A M Hunt Lieut Col RAMC O.C. 135th Field Ambulance	"

140/1315.

40th Divn.

135th Field Ambulance.

COMMITTEE FOR THE
MEDICAL HISTORY OF THE WAR
Date −9 DEC. 1916

Army Form C. 2118.

WAR DIARY or **INTELLIGENCE SUMMARY**

(Erase heading not required.)

135th Field Ambulance   Vol V Page 1

Place	Date	Hour	Summary of Events and Information	Remarks and references to Appendices
NOEUX LES MINES 36B/40000 L25.t.3-4	1916 Oct 1st	1.AM	Winter time adopted. Admissions O.R. Sick 16 - Wounded Officer 1, other ranks 5 - Evacuated Sick O.R. 5. Wounded Officer 2. O.R. 1 -	
	2nd		Admitted O.R. Sick 21. Officer 1 Wounded Officer 1. O.R. 4 - Evacuated - Sick Officer 1. O.R. 6 Wounded Officer 2 - O.R. 4	
"	3rd		Lieut R.N. CRAIG RAMC M.O. 13 Yorkshire Regt. admitted suffering from G.S.W. head (shell). Admissions Sick O.R. 39 including dental cases. Wounded Officer 2 - Evacuated Sick 15	
	4th		Lieut J.K DAVIES RAMC detailed to report to OC 13 Yorkshire Regt for duty in relief of Lieut R.N. CRAIG RAMC name recorded - Admission Sick 25 O.R. Wounded 1 - Evacuated Sick O.R. 9 Wounded Officer 2	
	5th		Admitted Sick O.R. 14 Wounded 1. Evacuated Sick 10 O.R. Wounded 2 - No. 81803 Pte WILLIAMS E.R - RAMC admitted for duty (reinforcement)	
	6th		Admitted - O.R. Sick 16 - Wounded Officer 2 O.R. 1 - Evacuated - Sick O.R. 7 - Wounded Officer 1 - O.R.1	
	7th		Admissions - Sick Officer 1 other ranks 23 - Wounded nil - Evacuated Officer Sick 1 - O.R. 6	

SECRET

Army Form C. 2118.

WAR DIARY - 135th Field Ambulance
or
INTELLIGENCE SUMMARY.
(Erase heading not required.)

Vol V page 2

Place	Date	Hour	Summary of Events and Information	Remarks and references to Appendices
NOEUX LES MINES	1916 October 6th	3 a.m	40 Div Op Order No 6 6/10/16 received to effect - right subsection MAROC sent to be handed over to 37th Division - 135 F.A. will hand over ADS at South MAROC to	
Hop 36 B 40/170	8th		49th Field Ambulance - relief to be completed by 3 a.m on 9th inst "	
-25. 6.34			Admission Sick O.R. 24. Wounded Officer 2 O.R. 4 - Evacuated - Sick O.R. 4 Wounded 1	
"	9th	1 pm	40 Div Op Order No 7 dated 9/10/16 - to effect 40 Div front is to be extended to include Hulluch Salient - 137 F.A. with temporarily take over ADS. at from 25th Field Ambulance & 8th Division relief to be completed at 6 pm 11th inst 137th F.A. will be relieved by 136th F.A on the LOOS - 14 BIS HULLUCH Sector and will take over 1st Corps Rest Station A Section LABEUVRIERE and Officers Rest Station at AIRE -	
"		3 pm	ADS to SOUTH MAROC handed over to 48th F.A. - Admitted Sick O.R.18. Wounded Officer 1. O.R.14. Evacuated Sick O.R 4 Wounded Officer 1 O.R.1	
"	10th		LIEUT- MALCOLM detailed to relieve LIEUT PATERSON as M.O. to 12th Suffolk Regt as temporary measure CAPT W SMITH - RANCE (T) reported for duty	

SECRET

WAR DIARY 135th Field Ambulance

or

INTELLIGENCE SUMMARY Vol V page 3

Army Form C. 2118.

Place	Date	Hour	Summary of Events and Information	Remarks and references to Appendices
NOEUX LES MINES	1916 Oct 10th cont		Admitted Sick O.R. (including dental cases) 24 - Wounded Officers 2. O.R. 1. evacuated O.R Sick 9 - Wounded Officer 1. O.R. 9.	
MAP 36P 1/40000 L.25.6.3.4	11th		Admitted O.R Sick 42 including Scabies 2, 1 S.W. - Wounded Officers 1 - O.R 4 Evacuated Sick O.R. 19 Wounded Officer 1.	
"	12th		Sent W.R.P MENEIGHT detached to relieve Lt PALMER RAMC on 17th & 11th K.O.R.L. Regt from 12th to 26th inst.	
			Took over charge of Divisional Baths MAZINGARBE	
			Capt. W.J.D ROBERTSON RAMC marked on completion of duty with 18th Cubra Hsp. -	
			Admissions - Officers Sick 2. O.R.12 - Wounded O.R. 2. Evacuated Sick O.R. 8. Wounded 6	
"	13th		No. 43941 B.Dr. O'HAGAN evacuated to No.1 C.C.S. suspected case of Dysentery Admissions Sick O.R. 15 Wounded Officers 1 O.R 4 Evacuated - Sick Officer 1 - O.R. 6 - Wounded Officer 1 - O.R 1	
"	14th		Admitted O.R Sick 20 including 1 S.W. Wounded Officer 1 Evacuated Sick O.R. 1 Wounded Officer 1. O.R. 2	

SECRET

Army Form C. 2118.

135 ᵗʰ Field Ambulance

WAR DIARY
or
INTELLIGENCE SUMMARY.
(Erase heading not required.)

Vol V. Page 4

Place	Date	Hour	Summary of Events and Information	Remarks and references to Appendices
NOEUX LES MINES	1916 Oct 15ᵗʰ		Admission Sick O.R. 9. Wounded O.R.1. Evacuated Sick O.R.8 - Wounded nil	
MAP B36 1 44.0.0.0 25.6.3.4	16ᵗʰ		2 N.C.Os & 18 men despatched to MAZINGARBE to work under Sanitary Officer 40ᵗʰ Divⁿ No 25.221 - Pte HARRIS F. Admitted & evacuated to No 6 C.C.S as a suspected case of Cerebro-Spinal Meningitis. (12ᵗʰ S.W.B.) Admitted Sick O.R.12 - Wounded O. Evacuated Sick O.R.9. Wounded 1	
	17ᵗʰ		Admitted Sick O.R. 32 (including 6 casuals for retention & evacuation) Wounded Officers 2. O.R. 11 - Evacuated Sick O.R.5. Wounded O.R.5. No 27595 Pte BARTER G - 18 Welsh & No 27569 Pte RILEY J 18 Welsh died of G.S.Wounds	
		9 p.m	No 35-85-9 Pte SPALDING F - 12ᵗʰ S.W.B sent in on suspected case of C.S.M. Transferred to No 7 Gen/Hosp MALASSISE -	
	18ᵗʰ		Admitted Sick Officers 1 O.R. 26 - Wounded O.R.4. Evacuated Sick & Wounded Officers 2 O.R.3. (4 hrs contact with Pte SPALDING admitted for observation)	
	19ᵗʰ		One German prisoner Pte GLIMERCK JOHANN - 35ᵗʰ Infantry Regt Admitted from 17 Potwl Cy Prisoners of War Camp DROUVIN - Inflpitigo	

SECRET

WAR DIARY or **INTELLIGENCE SUMMARY**
(Erase heading not required.)

135th Field Ambulance   Army Form C. 2118.

Vol V pages 5

Place	Date	Hour	Summary of Events and Information	Remarks and references to Appendices
NOEUX LES MINES MAP 36 B	1916 Oct 19th (1)		Admitted Sick O.R. 21. Wounded 2 - Evacuated Sick 5 - Wounded 4	
4070	20th		Admitted Sick O.R. 17. Wounded o.r. - Evacuated Sick O.R. 10 - Wounded 2	
S.L 63.4	21st	2.40pm	Wire received from O.C.21 Wilts Bearer Sub - reporting contact with one of C.S.M. Sugden	
			Admitted Sick O.R. 19. Wounded n/s - Evacuated Sick 15 O.R. Wounded Officer 1	
"	22 -		Admitted Sick O.R. 4. including 3 German Prisoners from Prisoner of War Camp. DROUVIN - Wounded Officer 1 - Sick Evacuated Officer 1. O.R.8 - Wounded n/s	
"	23rd	7h am	46th Division M.O.M.E. Operation Order no 8 dated 23-10-16 received. In effect this F.A. 40 = Division is to be relieved by the 24th Division and intercalated into G.H.Q. Reserve 135th = F.O. will be relieved by 72nd = F.O. on 27th inst; and will march to new area on the same date under orders of G.O.C. 120th Infy Bde. xxx All patients in hospital not evacuated will be handed over to relieving F.A. xxx Relief to be completed as soon as respective dealings xxx (F.D.S.; billets and emplacements to be handed over to admin. parties of incoming units under arrangements between O.C. concerned xxx - Admitted Sick Officer 1. O.R. 19 - Wounded Officer 1. Evacuated Sick O.R. 9 Wounded Officer 1	

SECRET

WAR DIARY
or
INTELLIGENCE SUMMARY
(Erase heading not required.)

Army Form C. 2118.

135th Field Ambulance

Vol V. page 6.

Place	Date	Hour	Summary of Events and Information	Remarks and references to Appendices
NOEUX LES MINES 36.B.4.d.7.7.	Oct 24th 1916		Lieut C.A. BURTS RAMC (T.C.) reported for duty and was taken on strength of unit – Admission – Sick OR 24. Wounded 1. Evacuated Sick OR 18. Wounded hit	
L.25.6.3.4	25th	9 a.m.	120th Inf Bde Operation Order No 39. 25/10/16 received to open "120th Inf Bde Wld march to billets in BRUAY on 27th Oct as per attached march Table " " + v	
"			135th F.A. will arrange for horse ambulance to march in rear of 14th Inf H.Q.'s midway between PETIT SAINS (R 2.c.5.4) at 10.30 a.m. 29½ and another to march at rear of 120 T.M. Battery. some undergone at 1 p.m.	
			Admission Sick OR 17. Wounded Officers 1 OR 2. Evacuated Sick OR 10 – Wounded 4	
	26th		Advance party of 72nd F.A. arrived to take over advance duties Admission – taken us Admission Sick OR 21 OR Wounded 3 – Evacuated Sick OR 18. Wounded 3 –	
"	27th		Handed over Main Dressing Station to 72nd F.A. Transferred Patients Officers Sick 2 OR 41 – Wounded 2	
			Ambulance marched off en route for BRUAY at 1 p.m.	
BRUAY BILLETS T.22.6.55	28th	4 p.m.	Arrived at billets 4 p.m. – Very hang rain	
			120th Inf Bde marched to billets in area A – Billeting party met Staff Capt at Coin Route J.15.b.5.4 at 7 a.m. – 135th F.A. found column at J.15. d.4.1. and	

WAR DIARY

SECRET

Army Form C. 2118.

135th Field Ambulance

Vol V Aug 7

Place	Date	Hour	Summary of Events and Information	Remarks and references to Appendices
	Oct 19/16			
	28th	9.30 a.m	marched behind 231st Field Co R.E. via HOUDAIN - BEUGIN - LA COMTE - HOUVELIN - ROCOURT - MONCHY BRETON - ORLENCOURT to ROCOURT - ST LAURENT - T.9.d.2.5	
ROCOURT ST LAURENT 36B T.9.d.2.5		4 p.m	Arrived at billets - T.9.d.2.5. Billets consist of farm house with vacant outbuildings - No arrangement whatever for sick - Very wet & muddy - Admitted at BRUAY & ROCOURT ST LAURENT. Sick O.R. 10 - transferred to CCS BRUAY & No.12 Stationary Hospital ST POL. 10 - Order from 120th Inf Bde issued to effect 120th Inf Bde Group will move to billets in "C" area on 29th Oct - 135th F.O. to remain at ROCOURT ST LAURENT (in "C" area)	
"	29th		Cleaning up billets very wet - Dear O.C. No.12 Stationary Hospital at St Pol re taking in cases sent to Ambulance - Admitted Sick O.R. 6 Transferred to No.12 Stationary Hosp. 6. O.R. sick - Officer of A.D.M.S. Close at BRAQUEMONT and open at ROELLECOURT (area C) at 10 A.M Oct 30th	
"	30th		A.D.M.S. visited billets - Admitted (in front this Ambulance) Sick Officer 2 O.R.B Transferred Officer 2 O.R. eight (to No.12 Stationary Hosp.)	
"	31st	9.30 a.m	120th Bde Orders issued to effect that Bde will move to billets in D area on 2nd November.	

T2134. Wt. W708-775. 500000. 4/15. Sir J. C. & S.

SECRET 135th Field Ambulance Army Form C. 2118.

WAR DIARY
or
~~INTELLIGENCE~~ SUMMARY.
(Erase heading not required.)

Vol V page 8

Place	Date	Hour	Summary of Events and Information	Remarks and references to Appendices
	Oct 31st 1916			
ROCOURT			Admitted - OR - 11 - Evacuated OR - 11 -	
ST LAURENT				
36B 40.70			A.M. Monk Lieut Col	
T.9.d.25			Name	
			O.C. 135th Field Ambulance	

140/862

40th Div.

135th Field Ambulance.

Nov. 1916

COMMITTEE FOR THE
MEDICAL HISTORY OF THE WAR
Date -3 JAN. 1917

Army Form C. 2118.

Scout 135 Field Ambulance

WAR DIARY
or
INTELLIGENCE SUMMARY.
(Erase heading not required.)

Vol VI Page I

Vol 6

Place	Date	Hour	Summary of Events and Information	Remarks and references to Appendices
ROCOURT ST LAURENT	1916 Nov 1st	8.30 p.m.	120th Infty Brigade Operation Order No 43 dated 1/11 received — to effect 120th Infy Bde Group will march to billets in Area D on 2nd November	
36B/40000			× × × 135 F.A. starting point ROELLECOURT CHURCH 9 am — cont	
T 9 d 2.5			FOUFFLIN RICAMETZ-TERNAS BURIEVILLE & SIBIVILLE Admitted Sick Officer 1 – O.R. 14 Evacuated Sick Officer 1 O.R. 14	
SIBIVILLE	2nd	11.45 am	Ambulance arrived SIBIVILLE – Sick transferred to No 6 Sta. Hospital FREVENT. Admitted Sick Officer 1 O.R. 10 – Evacuated Sick Officer 1 OR 10	
Map 10/100,000 Sun Sheet 3rd		6.30 a.m.	120th Infty Bde Op Order No 44 dated 3-11-16 to received – to effect 120th Infy Bde Group will march to billets in Area J on 4th November × The march will be continued to the BERNAVILLE area on the 5th inst – 135. F. A. starting point junction of FREVENT BONNIERS and FREVENT BOUQUEMAISON reach time 8.31 a.m. destination to be VILLERS L'HOPITAL. – Admitted OR Sick 7 Evacuated O.R sick 7 Ambulance marched at 7.15 am to destination arrived VILLERS L'HOPITAL at 10.25 a.m. to billet. Admitted Sick 8 – Evacuated OR OR 8	
VILLERS L'HOPITAL 50-000 Ord Sheet C. 4	4th	7 p.m	120th Infty Bde Order No 45 4/11 received to effect that 120 Infy Bde Group will march	

Army Form C. 2118.

WAR DIARY
or
INTELLIGENCE SUMMARY
(Erase heading not required.)

Scott 135th Field Ambulance

Vol VI page 2

Place	Date	Hour	Summary of Events and Information	Remarks and references to Appendices
			to billets in Area N on 5th November - 135th F.A. to H.S.q with AUTHIE by 8.45	
	Nov 5th	a.m.	units FROHEN LE GRANDE - FROHEN LA PETIT - LE MEILLARD - BERNAVILLE	
			DOMESMONT destination. LANCHES	
			Ambulances marched from VILLERS L'HOPITAL at 8 a.m.	
LANCHES		12 noon	Ambulance arrived at LANCHES 12 noon	
LENS SHEET 1 10000 B.5	6th		Admitted O.R. 18 - Evacuated O.R. 18	
			In billets - Billets fatigue - Med inspection but clothing etc	
		2 p.m.	Tried by Field Gen Court Martial of Sergt J. Tarpler O.S.C. attached 135 F.A. at Amb Head	
			quarters for drunkenness on line of march on 2nd inst	
			Admitted Sick O.R. 8 - Evacuated O.R. nil 8	
"	7th		Ground clearing up billets etc. Admission Sick O.R. 2 Evacuation O.R. 2.	
			Weather still content rain	
"	8th	2 p.m.	Promulgation on parade of finding & sentence of F.G.C.M. on Sergt Tarpler F.S.C.	
			Sentence to be reduced to ranks and six months imprisonment with hard labour	
			Admission Sick O.R. 11 - Evacuations Sick O.R. 11	

WAR DIARY
or
INTELLIGENCE SUMMARY

135th Field Ambulance

Vol VI page 3

Army Form C. 2118.

Place	Date	Hour	Summary of Events and Information	Remarks and references to Appendices
LANCHES	9th		Remain in billets LANCHES – Sick being evacuated to C.C.S. BEAUVAL. Weather improved. Admissions Sick O.R. 2 – Evacuations Sick O.R. 1.	
LENS Sheet B.5	10th		Still at LANCHES – Orders received from A.D.M.S. to effect that Bearer Division of Ambulance would take over from 49th Division on morning of 13th inst. Advanced Dressing Station HEBUTERN (K 9 d 3.3) Dug out for personnel at K 15 a 7.9. Work of HEBUTERNE and Advanced Dressing Station SALLY DELL (J 16-6 9-2). Bearer Division not to move till further notice. Admissions Sick Officers 2 O.R. 7 – Evacuations Officers 2 O.R. sick 8.	
	11th		Instructions to Bearer Division now cancelled – 120th Inf Bde. Op Order No 48 11/7/16 received to effect 120th Inf B.M. group will march to billets at DOULLENS on 12th November – 135 F.A. to remain – Further instructions – Admissions O.R. Sick 15 – Evacuations O.R. sick 15 – 135 F.A. received instructions to remain in present billets.	
	12th		Admitted – nil – Evacuated O.R. sick 1.	
	13th		Still at LANCHES – weather much better. Admissions nil – Evacuations nil	

WAR DIARY

135th Field Ambulance

Vol VI page 4

INTELLIGENCE SUMMARY

Place	Date	Hour	Summary of Events and Information	Remarks and references to Appendices
LANCHES MAP 100-575	14th		Admissions Sick OR 1 - Evacuated nil	
LENS SHEET B.5	15th	5.45 a.m	121st Infantry Brigade Order No 30 15/16 received - to effect that 121st B⁴⁵ group + 25 Div Supply Column and 135th F.A. will march this morning to AUXI-BEAUVOIR-BONNIERS-VILLERS L'HOPITAL-MEZEROLLES — 135 F.A and 25 Div Supply Column will billet in MEZEROLLES. Ambulance left LANCHES at 9 a.m via BERNAVILLE and found column at AUTHIEUX and MEZEROLLES - 1.30 p.m — (1 riding horse + 1 mule left on string) of MAIRE - LANCHES - lame — A.D.V.S 40 Div notified) Admission OR sick 1	
MEZEROLLES MAP 117-575 (LENS) D.4	16th		Billet cleaned up (taken over very dirty) Admitted Sick 1 OR Evacuated nil	
	17th	2 am	121st Inf B⁴⁵ Order 16/16 to effect that Brigade group (including 135 F.A.) will march tomorrow to ma BOUQUEMAISON-LE SOUICH 135 F.A starting from MEZEROLLES-DOULLENS ROAD at 9 am — Billets S.E portion of LE SOUICH Ambulance left MEZEROLLES 9 a.m arrived at billets LE SOUICH - 1.30 p.m Admissions Officers Sick 1 OR 10 - Evacuated Officers Sick 1 OR 10 —	

Army Form C. 2118.

WAR DIARY
or
INTELLIGENCE SUMMARY.
(Erase heading not required.)

Scott 135th Field Ambulance
Vol VI page 5

Place	Date	Hour	Summary of Events and Information	Remarks and references to Appendices
	1916 Nov			
LE SOUICH	18th		121st Inf Bde Orders 178 received last night 9pm to effect 121 Bde Group including 135 F.A. will march tomorrow to area SUS ST LEGER — WARLUZEL 135 F.A. starting point DOULLENS—FREVENT ROAD 12 noon to WARLUZEL (route posterior) Ambulance joined column at LE SOUICH at 11.30 am	
Map ref (LENS) E.4				
WARLUZEL (LENS 157775)	19th	3.30 pm	arrived WARLUZEL 3.30 pm, Billets ready all occupied turn left bed — Admitted Officers sick 1 — OR 2 — Evacuated Officers sick 1 OR 3 — Very heavy rain all night — Billets cleaned up and readjusted Admitted Officers sick 1 OR 7 — Evacuated Officers sick 1 — OR 7	
"	20th		Weather better, cleaning up billets continued — all damaged from wet kits now come to stamp received — old one destroyed — Admitted Officers sick 1 — OR nil Evacuated Officers sick 1 OR nil —————	
"	21		Lieut CABIRT's name left unit to take over duties of M.O. to 12th Suffolk Regt in relief of Lieut MALCOLM RAMC 120th Inf Bde Orders received to effect that 120 Inf Bde Group will march to billets on 22nd November 135 F.A. to ORVILLE — Time & route obtained Admitted Sick 8 — Evacuated 6 each other ranks	

Army Form C. 2118.

135th Field Ambulance
Vol VI page 6

WAR DIARY or INTELLIGENCE SUMMARY.
(Erase heading not required.)

Instructions regarding War Diaries and Intelligence Summaries are contained in F. S. Regs., Part II. and the Staff Manual respectively. Title pages will be prepared in manuscript.

Place	Date	Hour	Summary of Events and Information	Remarks and references to Appendices
ORVILLE	Nov 22nd 1916		Ambulance left WARLUZEL 10.30 a.m. arrived in billets Orville 3.30 p.m. Lieut J.K.DAVIES RAMC rejoined unit on completion of temporary duty with H.L. Infantry	
LENS 1/100000 E.5		9.30 p.m	120th Inf Bde Order dated 22/11 received to effect that Brigade Group will march to billets in the CANAPLES area on 23rd November - 135th F.A. to FIEFFES -	
			Admitted Sick OR - 2. Evacuated Sick OR 4	
FIEFFES	23		Ambulance left ORVILLE 9 a.m. arrived in billets FIEFFES 2.30 p.m. Lieut MALCOLM RAMC rejoined unit on completion of temporary duty with SUFFOLK REGT - Admitted Sick OR 21 - Evacuated OR Sick - 21.	
LENS 1/10000 C.6	24th		120th Inf Bde Order dated 23/11 received to effect 120th Inf Bde will move to billets 135th F.A. to GORENFLOS under BERNEUIL - DOMART - Left FIEFFES 10 a.m arrived in billets GORENFLOS 2.40 p.m Admitting Sick OR 9. Evacuated OR 9	
GORENFLOS 1/100000	25th		Very heavy rain - cleaning up billets - Sick evacuated to AMIENS	

Army Form C. 2118.

Scott 135th Field Ambulance

WAR DIARY
INTELLIGENCE SUMMARY
(Erase heading not required.)

Vol VI page 7

Place	Date	Hour	Summary of Events and Information	Remarks and references to Appendices
GORENFLOS	Nov 1916		Lieut J.K DAVIES left unit for temporary duty as O/C 83rd Sanitary Section	
Tents 100 O.Rs			Admitted O.R. Sick 19 – Evacuated Sick O.R. 17	
A.5			120th Inf Bgde orders dated 25/11 moved to effect Temp 120th M.G. Coy & 120th T.M.B. rode minus to billets in ALLIES & AILLY & 135 F.A to billets in FAMECHON on 26th November	
			Admitted Sick O.R. 19 – Evacuated Sick O.R. 17	
FAMECHON	26/11/16		Ambulance left GORENFLOS at 10 A.M. arrived in billets FAMECHON 12.15 P.M.	
Tents 100 O.Rs			Admitted Sick O.R. 18 Evacuated Sick O.R. 14 – Capt J. CRAWFORD rejoined from leave	
A.6	27/11/16		Cleaning up billeting area – Sub evacuated to AMIENS serum conc K ABBEVILLE – Admitted O.R. Sick 16 – Evacuated O.R. sick 10.	
"	28.		LIEUT-ALLINSON detailed on temporary Town Major FAMECHON billeting area – Shops & remts of billets prepared – billet accommodation return being made 0 funds of our N.C.Os & 10 men took over Brigade baths at BUSSUS BUSSUEL Admitted Sick Officers 1 – O.R. 10 evacuated O.R. sick 6	
"	29th		Billet improvements continued – weather very cold frosty & dump Admitted Sick O.R. 3 – Evacuated Officers sick 1 –	

WAR DIARY
or
INTELLIGENCE SUMMARY.

135th Field Ambulance

Army Form C. 2118.

VOL. VI page 8

Place	Date	Hour	Summary of Events and Information	Remarks and references to Appendices
FAMECHON	Nov 30th 1916		Cleaning up - overhauling equipment afting journal entries	
A-6				

R M Hunt Lieut Col RAMC
OC - 135th Field Ambulance

SECRET

Confidential
War Diary
of
135th Field Ambulance

from 1st December 1916 - to
31st December 1916 -

Volume VII

R N Hunt Lieut Col
Name
OC 135th Field
Ambulance

WAR DIARY
or
INTELLIGENCE SUMMARY

Army Form C. 2118.

135 Field Ambulance

Vol VII page 1

Place	Date	Hour	Summary of Events and Information	Remarks and references to Appendices
AMIECHON	Dec 1916 1st		Ambulance still in billets at FAMECHON – General cleaning up continued	
ENS?????			Admitted Sick O.R. 17 – Evacuated O.R. sick 6	
A.6.	2nd		– do – Admitted Sick Officer 1 O.R. 18. Evacuated sick 7.	
"	3rd		No change – Admitted – Sick O.R. 9 – Officer evacuated 1, O.R. 8	
"	4th		Capt W.R.P. M?NEIGHT rejoined unit on completion of leave	
"	5th		Admissions Sick O.R. 11 Evacuated Sick O.R. 12	
"			Instructions received from ADMS 40th Div to prepare for immediate move to take over huts at ???? from French Medicin-en-chef as a Corps	
"			Evening Station (Orders from 39 m.S. XV Corps)	
"			Admitted Sick O.R. 9 evacuated O.R. 7	
"	6th		Orders in corps to Corps cancelled by XV Corps	
"			Admitted Sick O.R. 2 – Evacuated O.R. sick 8 – Capt. ROBERTSON N?M?? proceeded to England on special leave – 120th Inf Bde Order No 58 6/12/16	
"	7th		recd – to effect that 120th & 13th Bde group will probably move to XV Corps Middle Area – Transport by road to St SAUVEUR on 14th Dec. Remr ? Middle Area on 15th = Remrs from Area 6 to XV Corps Middle Area by train on 15th inst	

WAR DIARY

135th Field Ambulance Army Form C. 2118.

Sunt _____ Vol VII pages 2

INTELLIGENCE SUMMARY.

(Erase heading not required.)

Place	Date	Hour	Summary of Events and Information	Remarks and references to Appendices
AMIE CLEON	1916 Dec 7th		Admitted O.R. sick 2 Evacuated O.R. sick 4	
ENS	8th		Lieut J K DAVIES R.A.M.C. reported on completion of Leave duty with 83rd San Section and proceeded on 14 days leave on renewal of contract 40 Div R.A.M.C. Order No. 13 8/12 u nov of 9 units wound — Admitted Sick	
A.6	9th		O.R. 9 wounded O.R. sick 5 120th Inf Btn Order No. 59 dated 9/12/16 wound u nov Camps 111 and 112 Mngr of ALBERT forms L.2.b.5 J ARBRE FOUCHE line from Allother & 120th Inf Btn group — Admitted O.R. nov 17 - Evacuated O.R. sick 7	
"	"		Admitted Sick O.R. 7 - Evacuated O.R. sick 8	
"	10th			
"	11th		On N.C.O. reported to Staff Captain 120th Btn a LUNGPRE LES CORPS SAINTS Lieut as admin hunter to proceed to formed cover — Admitted Officer Sick 2 — O.R. 4	
"	12th		2 Other ranks 12 - Evacuated Officer Sick 2 - O.R. 4 Inf Btn Order No. 60 12/12 rec) to effect removal of 120 Inf Btn will march to Gillette on 14th inst — 135th F.A. to MOUFLERS — Admitted Sick Officer 2 O.R. 11 - Evacuated Officer 2 Other Ranks 11 -	

WAR DIARY or INTELLIGENCE SUMMARY

Army Form C. 2118.

135th Field Ambulance — Vol VII pages 3

Place	Date	Hour	Summary of Events and Information	Remarks and references to Appendices
	Dec			
FAMECHON	13		Transport of Unit marched at 9.45 a.m. to join Brigade Transport Column en route for ST SAUVEUR (1st half for night) — Admitted Officers 2. O.R. 38	
			Transport left ST SAUVEUR en route for VAUX SUR SOMME (2nd half for night)	
			Personnel of Ambulance marched to billets at MOUFLERS — Admitted Sick 2	
MOUFLERS	14			
	15		Left MOUFLERS at 5.45 a.m. marched to LONGPRE LES CORPS. Entrained at 7.30 a.m. in Troop Train No 2 with 2 cols + 120th Inf Bde around EDGEHILL Station (DERNANCOURT) 1 p.m. — marched to Camp 112 — L.2.B — (S. of ARBRE FOURCHE) took over from huts for personnel + hospital accommodation	
Camp 112 map ALBERT 57D.S.E. L.2.6.			Transport arrived from VAUX SUR SOMME — 4 a.m. Main Ambulance arrived 9 p.m. (Admitted nil — Evacuation to AMIENS O.R. sick 2)	
	16		Inspecting and cleaning of camp — Return ammunition + equipment Admitted O.R. sick 4 evacuated nil.	
"	17 "		Do " do " Admitted S.O.R. 5 — Evacuated O.R. sick 4 Under orders from A.D.M.S. Lieut B.P. ALLINSON left the Unit to take over duties of 17th Welsh left	

WAR DIARY or **INTELLIGENCE SUMMARY**

Army Form C. 2118.

135th Field Ambulance

Vol VII page 4

Place	Date	Hour	Summary of Events and Information	Remarks and references to Appendices
Camp 112	Dec 18.		Still improving camp. Admission OR sick 7. Evacuated Sick 4. to 2/2 London CCS & 34 CCS GROVETOWN	
MAR-	19		Lieut McNEIGHT attached as MO to 40 Div Am Column as a Company worked to & from this camp — Admission Sick OR 14 — Evacuated OR 9	
4.2.b	20th		Intimation rcd from 4.2. 126th Inf Bde that Bde group will relieve the regue Bde group of 33rd Div on night of 26/27th Dec. Admitted OR sick 9. — Evacuated OR sick 5	
ALBERT	21st			
"	22nd		Proceeded to Camp 17. SUZANNE & arrange details of relief with OC 99th F.A. visited ADS & Bearer posts at MARICAS LE FOREST and LE GRANIER — Admitted OR Sick 24 — Evacuated Sick OR 12. —	
"	23rd		NAMC 40 Div Of Order No 13 dated 23/12/16 received — to effect that 135 F.O. will relieve 99th F.A. Taking over ADS and Bearer Posts on 26th & 27th inst	
"	24th		Arrangements for Advanced section to be made before OC concurred — Admitted 14 sick Evacuated 12 Admitted OR 9. Evacuated OR sick 11 —	
"	25th		Christmas Day. Admitted sick Officer 1 OR 14. Evacuated Officer 1 OR 21	

WAR DIARY or **INTELLIGENCE SUMMARY**

Army Form C. 2118.

of 135th Field Ambulance   Vol VII page 5

Place	Date	Hour	Summary of Events and Information	Remarks and references to Appendices
CAMP 112	Sept 26th		Advance party of 45 N.C.O. men under command of Capt Crawford-Nance sent in motor and horsed ambulances with necessary equipment to take over Advanced Dressing Station & Bearer Posts from 99th F.A. — Admitters O.R. Sick 6 wounded	
ALBERT 1/40000 L2.b	27th		OR Sick 6. Waggons parked. Remainder of relief party for A.D.S. Bearer posts 56 N.C.O. men dispatched in motor lorries to MARIPAS. Remainder of Ambulance marched at 10 a.m. for new Head Quarters at Camp 6	
CAMP 17	28th		17 SUZANNE — Took over two huts for personnel also 17 — Ambulance trein 2 Bearers 2 (from Camp 112). Visited A.D.S. — Pinney's Post (MARIPAS) B.15 a.6.7 and Bearer Post Le Forest B.16 a.4.6. Bearer Post LE GRANIERE B.16.c.8.7 and Bearer Post ANDOVER PLACE C.13 a.8.0. 120th Inf. Bde. in Right Sub. — Two battalions front — All sick and wounded evacuated to Corps Main Dressing Station MARICOURT — Capt. I.K. DAVIES	
SUZANNE from ALBERT 1/40000 G.6.6.8.4			reported unit on completion of tour.	
"	29th		Capt DAVIES returned for duty as MO to h.i. section 40th F.A.C. in a Company manner — Very heavy rain continued	

WAR DIARY of 135th = Field Ambulance

Army Form C. 2118.

Vol VIII Augs 6

Place	Date	Hour	Summary of Events and Information	Remarks and references to Appendices
Camp 17	Dec 30th 1916		Visited found area including Brim Park and Regt Aid Posts – Trenches in very bad state owing to enemia rain – Communication trenches impassable in many places	
SUZANNE			141 Div. front through A.D.S. about 50 cases of early "Trench foot" practically all carrying done astride trenches – all cases evacuated to Corps Main Dressing Station (10 ¾ A) all walkable motor ambulances used	
ALBERT 40.070				
28.68.4	31st		120th Inf Bdes to be relieved by 121st Brigade Tonight	

M.H. Muat Lieut Col RAMC
OC 135th
Field Ambulance

140/9+3

40. D.

135th Field Ambulance

COMMITTEE FOR THE
MEDICAL HISTORY OF THE WAR
Date 13 MAR. 1917

SECRET

Army Form C. 2118.

Instructions regarding War Diaries and Intelligence Summaries are contained in F.S. Regs., Part II. and the Staff Manual respectively. Title pages will be prepared in manuscript.

WAR DIARY
or
INTELLIGENCE SUMMARY.
(Erase heading not required.)

135ᵗʰ = Field Ambulance

Vol VIII pag. 1

Place	Date	Hour	Summary of Events and Information	Remarks and references to Appendices
	1917			
Camp nr SUZANNE	Jan 1ˢᵗ		Headquarters at Suzanne, Brain Post - PINNEY'S POST B.15.a.6.4. Brain Post	
ALBERT 4.pm			LE FOREST B.16.a.4.8. - A.D.S. LE CRANIER B.16.C.8.7. - A.D.S. ANDOVER PLACE C.13 a.8.0	
G.B.f.9.4.			During afternoon of 31ˢᵗ Dec 1916 a party of 120 M.G. Coy were heavily shelled near ANDOVER Capt CRAWFORD R.A.M.C. took a party of stretcher bearers and attended to wounded shell while fire was still going on - he was knocked over by the explosion of a shell and remained in deep hole but continued dressing wounded who because till all were was removed -	
	2ⁿᵈ		Reports of cases of trench foot among this A.D.S. much less	
	3ʳᵈ		Lieut J.K. DAVIES detailed to take over station of M.O.E. 17ᵗʰ Welsh Regt in relief of Lieut B.R. ALLINSON who returned for duty into Ambulance Lieut B. COHEN joined unit for duty	
	4ᵗʰ		Curtailment of Communication trench lead up to front area necessitating carrying on tph - Arrangements made for carrying up returns to A.D.S. ambulance by Brigade Mule Corny Capt CRAWFORD relieved by Lieut ALLINSON at ANDOVER	

SECRET

135=th Field Ambulance

WAR DIARY
or
INTELLIGENCE SUMMARY.

Army Form C. 2118.

Vol. VIII Page 2.

Place	Date	Hour	Summary of Events and Information	Remarks and references to Appendices
Headquarters Camp 17	1917 Jan 5th		Two officers field & ADS – LE CRANIERE and two & ANDOVER PLACE, found working on account of numbers of gun reports. Sick duty from units in reserve.	
SUZANNE			Num M.O. on in front line	
ALBERT 4078	6th		Capt. CRAWFORD admitted to No 34 C.C.S. for removal of splints of shell from head	
29.G.B.4			Capt. PROCTER R.A.M.C. joined unit for duty – was detailed for Temporary duty with 137 F.A. (Ambulance in reserve area) Improvement in clay site to	
			ammunition at ADS. & bearer posts continued	
	7th		Arrangements made for supplying hot tea, cocoa & soup at ANDOVER for men coming out of trenches – this is found to be very useful and provides many extricated men from becoming casualties	
	8th		Conditions for evacuating from front line much the same. Work continued on communication lines	
	9th		No 41898 L/Sgt. W.R. COLES – of this unit was severely wounded by a shell at night bearer post, he died at Corps Main Dressing Station shortly after admission. Instruction received from ADMS to take over and supervise a hut (C.I.) in Camp 21 for carrying out Prophylactic measures against "Trench foot"	

SECRET

WAR DIARY or **INTELLIGENCE SUMMARY**
(Erase heading not required.)

135th Field Ambulance   Vol VIII Page 3.

Army Form C. 2118.

Place	Date	Hour	Summary of Events and Information	Remarks and references to Appendices
	1919			
Budgm	Jun		Preparation of hut & mapping of trenches and carrying plan with French troops continues	
Camp 17	10th		Concretion informed in the evacuation trenches up the line	
SUZANNE	11th		Provision evacuation against Trench Foot commenced for Brigade in Reserve at	
Camp ALBERT			Camp 21 (121st Bde) – Provision Washing hut fitted with botreles and drying stoves	
4 – – – 9			recently working with consignments off troops - clothing first - Orders with Complies and	
4 8 8 4			Tale Powder	
	12th		Two private reinforcements arrived	
	13th		Large line of whole out suffering diminished for men leaving Complies Stoves & provision	
			washout for provision of Trench feet	
	14th		Conditions up the line normal – very few evacuation for G.S. Wounds – Trench	
			foot line – No 091093 Pte DUCAT A.S.C. attached to this unit was removed	
			wounded at BRAY by a splinter of shell unwashed to be 24 C.C.S.	
	15th		Capt CRAWFORD R.a.M.C. was evacuated with Medical him by the C in C for him	
			gallant conduct on 31st Dec 1916 the names of seven men mentioned with him	
			were mentioned in G.O Divisional Orders of that date –	
			Capt W SMITH R.a.M.(T) departed for England on Transfer to Home Establishment	

SECRET
Army Form C. 2118.

135 (H) Field Ambulance

WAR DIARY
or
INTELLIGENCE SUMMARY.
(Erase heading not required.)

Vol VIII Aug 4

Place	Date	Hour	Summary of Events and Information	Remarks and references to Appendices
	1917			
Headquarters	2am		Arrangements made for supplying Divisional Station to unit from ADS	
Camp 17	16		LE CRANIER —	
SUZANNE	17th		Three NCOs of this unit proceed to England having been accepted as Candidates for Temporary Commissions in Infantry	
NR ALBERT	18th		Usual routine work	
HUTS	19th		Lieut D. Martin A. W. & R.D. proceed to England on Special leave	
6.6.8.4			40th Divison RAMC Order No 15 1917 issued to effect that 8th Division is to relieve 40th Division in BOUCHAVESNES Sector on night 26/27 Division and 135 F.O. to hand over ADSs and Bearer Posts in BOUCHAVESNES Sector to advance section of 24th F.A. on 26th inst — one Tented Foot Prevention Hut at Camp 21 & 26th F.A. — F.A. to be brigaded with 120th Inf Bde for purpose of march and billeting	
	20th		Much trouble experienced with Motor Ambulance Cars owing to condition of Roads in advanced area — fires now in movement No	
	21st		Very hard frost. The last few days — Conditions for carrying patients improved	

SECRET

Army Form C. 2118.

WAR DIARY
or
INTELLIGENCE SUMMARY.
(Erase heading not required.)

135th Field Ambulance

Vol VIII – Aug 5 –

Place	Date	Hour	Summary of Events and Information	Remarks and references to Appendices
	1919			
Hudyn	Jan 22nd		Heavy frost continues Capt. A.J.C. TINCEY A.M.C. posted to Ambulance	
Camp 17			Report on promotion submitted for "Iamich fort" 2nd to A.D.M.S.	
SUZANNE	23rd		Frost continues. Number of cases been fort 15 during this ADS much less	
Camp ALBERT	24th		Tote Oct 24th F.O. ___ and O.B.S. Burns Park	
4TTD	25th		Handed over Trench fort function Unit C1 at Camp 25 to 26th Field Ambulance	
B.C.B.4	26th		Capt R PROCTER detailed to temporary duty with 11th Kings from (R) Senior MO	
			Lieut B.COHEN " " " 13th Yorks	
	26th		Handed over Advanced Dressing Station at BOUCHAVESNES Sector to 24th Field	
			Ambulance 8th Division - Personnel returned to Headquarters Camp 17 SUZANNE	
			Capt J CRAWFORD A.M.C. reported unit from 34th C.C.S. for duty	
CORBIE	27th		Ambulance moved from SUZANNE to CORBIE - transport by rail. Personnel by	
			Motor Lorries - Ambulance located in empty dwellings - CORBIE Accommodation	
AMIENS / 10.0 TD	28th		preparing for billeting in billets	
C - 1			Special clearing up - Orderly Ambulance Officers and O.R. 9 Evacuated officers 0	
			O.R. nil -	
	29th		Jay. Returns being clear up. - a large number of men writing own from duties	

Army Form C. 2118.

135= Field Ambulance

Vol VIII Page 6

WAR DIARY
or
INTELLIGENCE SUMMARY

SECRET

(Erase heading not required.)

Place	Date	Hour	Summary of Events and Information	Remarks and references to Appendices
CORBIE	1917 Jan 29th		and units orderly Division Chunlin Officer 1. O.R. 38 - Evacuated (It & CCS) Officers 1. O.R. 28	
AMIENS 10000 G-1	30th		Unit still continues - Transport vehicles being cleaned and overhauled - 2 horses and 2 N.C.O. men sent to Town Sanitary Officer Amiens. Officers 1. O.R. 23. Evacuated O.1. O.R. 19.	
	31st		Cold frosty weather still continues with some snow - Admitted - Officers 1. O.R. 45 - Evacuated Officers 1. O.R. 18 - Instructions received from D.M.S. XIV Corps re transfer of Unit to Corps Main Dressing Station MARICOURT & Corps Rest Station & CCS.	

31/1/17

A M Hunt Lieut Col
Name
O.C. 135= Field Ambulance

140/991

40 Am.

135th Field Ambulance.

COMMITTEE FOR THE
MEDICAL HISTORY OF THE WAR
Date 4- APR. 1917

SECRET

WAR DIARY
or
INTELLIGENCE SUMMARY.
(Erase heading not required.)

Army Form C. 2118.

135th Field Ambulance
Vol IX page 1

Place	Date	Hour	Summary of Events and Information	Remarks and references to Appendices
CORBIE (SOMME)	1917 4W 1st		40th Div. R.A.M.C. Order No 16 dated 28/12 received instruction to effect Trans. 40th Divn. (less Artillery) to G.H.Q. Reserve from 29th January – Do to to ready to entrain	
AMIENS map 10.000			at LONGUEAU & SALEUX 47 hrs after receipt of order. Hand fitting executive containers – Discharging equipment horses – obtaining its continued	
C.1	2nd		Admitted Officers nil O.R. Evacuated & Transferred Officer O.R. Tele received from A.D.M.S. in continuation of R.A.M.C. Order No 16 situation probable move to entraining station or receipt of order.	
"	3rd		N.O.M.C. detailed for temporary duty attached to this unit from 29-1-17 Lieut P.B. ALLINSON Interpreter Pernon Maurice attached to this unit with IV Corps Main Dressing Station Admitted Officers nil O.R. 33 Evacuated Off. nil O.R. 13.	
	4th		Service first continues – Admitted Officers 1 – O.R. 16 – Evacuated Off. 1 – O.R. 3	
	5th		It.Col A.W. Mont Name proceeded on 10 days leave to England – Capt W. Robertson took on temporary command of Ambulance – Lieut. Dr. Mr. A.W. Ward reported on completion of leave – Admitted Officers 1 – O.R. 28 – Evacuated O nil – O.R. 5.	
	6th		Capt. Crawford R.A.M.C. detailed for temporary duty as M.O. & S.A.A. portion of 40th D.A.C. Admitted Officers nil O.R. 25 – Evacuated Officers nil O.R. 10 –	

SECRET

135th Field Ambulance

Vol IX — Page 2 —

WAR DIARY or INTELLIGENCE SUMMARY

Army Form C. 2118.

Place	Date	Hour	Summary of Events and Information	Remarks and references to Appendices
CORBIE (SOMME)	1917 Feb 6th		Further details re front, now 8 Division at 47 hour notice received.	
	7th		First Ambulance Admission – Officers 4 – Other Ranks 27 – Evacuated Officers 4 OR.12	
Camp Amiens	8th		40th Division RAMC Order No 17 dated 8/2/17 received — to effect 40th Div. will relieve 8th Div. in RANCOURT Sector on 11/12 Feb x x x	
10.0.00				
Q.1.			135th F.O. will march from CORBIE to Camp 111 on 10th inst 2 G. Coys.	
			112 on 11th inst and will arrange for accommodation of selfs in these camps and Sanitary supervision of them Areas in conjunction with Camp Commandant	
			Admitted Officers 4 – OR.25 – Evacuated Officers 4 – OR.12	
	9th		All cases in hospital transmitted to C.C.S. C.A.S. on duty owing to move	
			Admitted Officers – nil – OR.17 – Evacuated O. nil OR.16	
CAMP 111	10th		Ambulance marched from J. McAdam CORBIE in full marching order via CORBIE BRAY road to Camp 111 – arrived 7.30 P.M.	
—			Capt J. CRAWFORD RAMC detained for duty at Divisional Oxford ALLERY	
			Admitted 0.5 – OR.44 Evacuated 0.5 – OR.52	
CAMP 112	11th		Ambulance moved to Camp 112 – Admitted 0.3 OR.11 Evacuated 0.3 OR.10	
Camp ALBERT	12th		General cleaning up of billets and surrounding Weather changing slight thaw	
1/40000 L.2.b.				

SECRET

Army Form C. 2118.

135th Field Ambulance

Vol IX Page 3

WAR DIARY or INTELLIGENCE SUMMARY.
(Erase heading not required.)

Place	Date	Hour	Summary of Events and Information	Remarks and references to Appendices
Camp 112	1917 Feb		and fall of snow — Admitted Officer nil. O.R. 6. Evacuated — O. nil — O.R. nil	
Camp ALBERT	12th			
	13th		Arrangements made & huts prepared for Trench foot prevention treatment for men in Camps 111-112. — Admitted Officer nil — O.R. 17 — Evacuated O. nil O.R. 1. Lieut COHEN. N&MC reported unit on completion of temporary duty with 13 York & Lanc Rgt	
40 OBS L. 2. C	14th		Admission O. 2. O.R. 24 — Evacuated Officer 2. O.R. 4. Snow set in — Admitted Officer 2 — O.R. 18 Evacuated Officer 2 O.R. nil	
	15th		Completed inspection of Small box respirators & Gas Helmets P.H. Admitted Officer nil O.R. 33 Evacuated Officer nil O.R.	
	16th		Snow continues with much rain and consequent mud — Admitted Officer nil O.R. 18 — Evacuated Officer nil O.R. 2 Capt R. PROCTOR reported unit off L/5 temporary duty with K.O.R.L. Regt	
	17th			
	18th		Arrangements completed for carrying out Trench foot prevention treatment. Lieut Col R.N.Hugh reported from here & resumed command of unit. Order received from A.D.M.S. that one complete tent subdivision is to take over Corps Scabies Station from 12th Field Ambulance on 20th inst	

SECRET   135th Field Ambulance   Army Form C. 2118.

WAR DIARY
or
INTELLIGENCE SUMMARY.
(Erase heading not required.)

Vol IX Page 4

Place	Date	Hour	Summary of Events and Information	Remarks and references to Appendices
Camp 112	July 19th		Went to CHIPILLY to arrange Tubing our Corps Station from 12th F.A. Admitted officers 2 O.R. 17. Evacuated officers 2 O.R —	
Camp ALBERT 40.d.6.0	20th		Tent Subdivision of C Section proceeded to Corps Section Station to take over. Capt R PROCTER (in command) + Lieut B COHEN. Admitted officers nil O.R 31. Evacuated officers — O.R 1	
L.2.b	21st		Three fout treatments continued — Capt A.J.C TINGEY name joined ambulance for duty — Admitted officers 1 - O.R 41 Evacuated officers — O.R 1	
"	22nd		Under orders from ADMS Capt McNEIGHT & Capt TINGEY were attached + proceeded to Corps Main Dressing Station MARICOURT for temporary duty. Admitted officers 2 O.R 23. Evacuated officers nil O.R nil	
"	23rd		Instructions received from DDMS XIV Corps that 135th Field Amb has first entitlement at Corps Station into which the new XIV Corps Rest Station at SAILLY LAURETTE from no 14 F.A. Admitted officers — O.R 23 Evacuated officers nil O.R nil	
"	24th		Proceeded to Camp 125 who assumed duty of from Sept to arrange	

Army Form C. 2118.

WAR DIARY
or
INTELLIGENCE SUMMARY.
(Erase heading not required.)

Sent. 135th Field Ambulance VOL IX page 5

Place	Date	Hour	Summary of Events and Information	Remarks and references to Appendices
Camp 112	Feb 24th 1916		Attack of influ - Report on Trench foot amongst Tunnellers furnished to D.D.M.S. Australian Division. Evacuating Officer O.R.	
	25th		Orders received from Headquarters XV Corps that 135 F.A. will move to Corps Rest Station on 26th and in relief of 19 F.A. 33rd Division Australian Division F.R. Evacuating Officer M.R.	
	26th		Capt ROBERTSON with detachment of 12 other ranks left 1st Camp 112 & Camp in Detention tent & Ambulance tent Formation Evacuating line for Tanks in Camps 111 & 112 — Remainder of Ambulance marched to SAILLY LAURETTE at 12.30 p.m. passed Camp 125 at 4 p.m.	
Camp 126			Taking over from the 19 F.A. Capt M. NEIGHT & TINGEY joined on Corps	
SAILLY LAURETTE	27th		Corps Rest Station v. Capt Junb COHEN from Corps Rest Station.	
Camp ALBERT 135 F.A. 6-5			19th F.A. handed over & marched from Camp 126 to Corps Dress Dressing Station = MARICOURT — Detachment of 135 F.A. doing duty at Corps Rest Station allotted to 135 F.A.	
	28th			
			J.H. Hunt Lieut Col Rgmt OC 135 F.A.	

140/2086

135th F.A.

COMMITTEE FOR THE
MEDICAL HISTORY OF THE WAR
Date −6 JUN. 1917

SECRET

Army Form C. 2118.

Instructions regarding War Diaries and Intelligence
Summaries are contained in F. S. Regs., Part II.
and the Staff Manual respectively. Title pages
will be prepared in manuscript.

WAR DIARY
or
INTELLIGENCE SUMMARY.
(Erase heading not required.)

135th Field Ambulance

VOL X Page 1

Vol 10

Place	Date	Hour	Summary of Events and Information	Remarks and references to Appendices
Corbie	1919 March 1st		Complete taking over of XV Corps Rest Station yesterday – No y Instructs taken over 728 – Detachments of one Officer & 30 men on Corps	
HILLY			Section Station CHIPILLY – and one Officer and 16 O.R. running est Camps	
LORETTE				
MAR ALBERT	4th		112 for our of best case and running Truck Inst Inst – Lieut B.P. ALLINSON rejoined unit on discharge from 38 C.C.S. –	
40 pts				
J 36	5th		Lieut B. COHEN detached for duty on M.O. to 17 Welsh Regt (Tenbury)	
c. 8.4	7th		No y Instructs running 729 – Quantities 23 & duty 36 – CCS.19.	
"	10th		Position as before – Capt C.B. RICHARDSON R.A.M.C. attached for transport duty – Canteen started for Camps – Capt. ROBERTSON and detachment from Camp 112 (1 on. 3 orderlies) rejoined unit	
"	12th		Ps 91820 Corp & Pte RAMC dispatched acting twin surgn with pray Ps 96035 a/L/Cpl W H LESTER dispatched acting S/Cpl into pray No y comm in Rest Station 707. Sicknesses 48 – & duty 32 – C.C.S. 15	
	14th			

SECRET

135th Field Ambulance   Army Form C. 2118.
vol. X   Pages 2

WAR DIARY
or
INTELLIGENCE SUMMARY
(Erase heading not required.)

Instructions regarding War Diaries and Intelligence Summaries are contained in F.S. Regs., Part II. and the Staff Manual respectively. Title pages will be prepared in manuscript.

Place	Date	Hour	Summary of Events and Information	Remarks and references to Appendices
Camp 12.5	1917 March 15th		No 75031 S/Sgt J COLLEY appointed to No 4 General Base Depot for transfer to R.E.	
AILLY			No 56732 Staff Sergt G. LORD - transferred to No 13. C.C.S	
LORETTE			Two N.C.O. sent to Divisional Anti Gas School for course of instruction	
NIAP			40 Div R.A.M.C orders No 19. 16/3/17 received	
ALBERT	19th			
	20th		Ground visited in Bryan Rd & Pretoret in Station 717 - Ambulance 32. on duty 29 CCS. 6	
J. 36	21st		40 Div R.A.M.C order No 20 20/3/17 received	
C. 8.4	22nd		Capt. C.B. RICHARDSON R.A.M.C. left unit for duty with 136th F.A.	
	24th		Summer time adopted 11 h.m	
	25th		40 Div R.A.M.C Orders No. 21. 22 dated 24/3/17 received	
	26th		No 6 Corps in Rest Station H.Q. - Ambulance 50 Duty 49. CCS 8.13	
	27th		No 75031 S/Sgt J COLLEY + No 71655 S/Sgt W H FOLLEY appointed acting Corporals with pay	

2353 Wt. W2544/1454 700,000 5/15 D. D. & L. A.D.S.S./Forms/C. 2118.

SECRET   Army Form C. 2118.

135th Field Ambulance

WAR DIARY
or
INTELLIGENCE SUMMARY.
(Erase heading not required.)

Vol. I Aug. 8

Instructions regarding War Diaries and Intelligence Summaries are contained in F.S. Regs., Part II and the Staff Manual respectively. Title pages will be prepared in manuscript.

Place	Date	Hour	Summary of Events and Information	Remarks and references to Appendices
	1917			
CAMP 125	Month 29th		Routine work as before at XV Corps Rest Station & XV Corps Lesion Station. No in Station 697 - Admitted 56 - duty 47 C.C.S. 17	
BAILLY LORETTE	31st			
MAP			No. of cases slightly wounded returned to duty during month 25	
ALBERT			No. of cases of Constitutes sick returned to duty during month 1040 —	
40.S.E. J.36. 8.4				

J M Minch Lieut Col
Name
OC 135th Field Ambulance

140/2026

165th F.A.

COMMITTEE FOR THE
MEDICAL HISTORY OF THE WAR
Date -6 JUN.1917

SECRET

Army Form C. 2118.

135th Field Ambulance

WAR DIARY
or
INTELLIGENCE SUMMARY
(Erase heading not required).

Vol XI App 1

Place	Date	Hour	Summary of Events and Information	Remarks and references to Appendices
CAMP 125 BAILLEULMONT	April 1st 1917		Ambulance still working XV Corps Rest Station and XV Corps Scabies Station —	
			Meeting of 4th Army Medical Society held at this Station —	
	3rd		Capt B.H. PALMER. RAMC posted to this unit whilst on patrol at IV Corps Offrs	
MAP ALBERT 1/40000			Rest Station on 30-3-17. 2 Turkish Offrs Strength Gains on Evacuation to Base	
	6th		Patients remaining 703 — admitted 38 — to duty 34 — to CCS 19	
	7th		40 O.W. R.A.M.C. Reinfs No 24 (Scotts) received (not affecting this unit) dated 4-4-17	
J.35			Rtnres as word. no 78031 a/S/Cpl J COLLEY granted a/Airport from 13-3-17 —	
6.5	9th		Capt B.P. ALLINSON RAMC proceeded to England on 14 days leave on renewal of	
			contract	
	11th		No. of Patients remaining 691 — admitted 34 — to duty 47 — to CCS 12 —	
			Whilst siting Gov't House found near here, hrs. A.P.M. & Area Commandant notified &	
			arrangement made for returning —	
	14th		Brosher as word. No. of Patients remaining 703. admitted 31- to duty 37- CCS 10	
	16th		Capt J. CRAWFORD RAMC rejoining on completion of temporary duty with 46th	
			Divisional School	
	19th		Capt W.R.P. McNEIGHT proceeded to England on 10 days Special leave —	

SECRET

WAR DIARY
INTELLIGENCE SUMMARY

135th Field Ambulance   Army Form C. 2118.

Vol. XI Page 2

Place	Date	Hour	Summary of Events and Information	Remarks and references to Appendices
	1917			
Camp 125 SAILLY	April 20th		Routine Work of unit as before. Patients remaining in Corps Rest Station 456 – Admitted 59 – to duty 53 – C.C.S. 18 –	
LAURETTE MAP ALBERT 1/40,000	23rd		40 E Ormond N.A.M.C. Order No 24 (ninth) dated 23-4-17 received (does not affect this unit)	
	25th		Capt. A.J.C. TINGEY R.A.M.C. (T.C.) left for England on expiration of contract and in strength of the unit	
			Capt. F.G. THATCHER R.A.M.C. placed on strength of unit. Has remained for Temporary duty with 137th Field Ambulance –	
J.35 6.6.5	26th		Capt. B.P. ALLINSON. rejoined unit on completion of intellect leave –	
	27th		Routine as before. Patients remaining 455 – admitted 71 – admitted 68 – C.C.S. 4 Owing to XV Corps Reinforcement Depot being moved to forward area at QUINCONCE Column. arrangements & duties are now sent to PLATEAU –	
	29th		Orders received from D.D.M.S. XV Corps to effect – Corps Rest Station at Camp 125 SAILLY LAURETTE will close at an early date. No 135 Field Ambulance will move to MARICOURT	

SECRET

WAR DIARY
INTELLIGENCE SUMMARY

135th Field Ambulance
Vol III page 3

Army Form C. 2118.

Place	Date	Hour	Summary of Events and Information	Remarks and references to Appendices
	April			
Camp 126 SAILLY LAURETTE	29th 1917		and take over the present Corps Main Dressing Station which will become the new Corps Rest Station " & "the Corps Sentence Station" will shortly move to MARICOURT under arrangements to be detailed later. Under instructions from DDMS III Corps 25 other ranks of the unit proceeded to Corps Main Dressing Station MARICOURT to relieve similar party of 26th F.A. and to	
MAP ALBERT				
57d				
35. b.6.5	30th		near Corps Main Dressing Station (at V.18.c Sheet 57c.) Weather conditions much improved last two days warm & sunny – Arrangements made for disinfecting old blankets – Remaining 75ft – Admissions 49 & duty 40 – C.C.S. 8.	

J M Monk Lieut. Col. R.A.M.C.
OC 135th Field Ambulance

May 1917.

No. 135. F.A.

COMMITTEE FOR THE
MEDICAL HISTORY OF THE WAR
Date 10.IIII.1917

SECRET

Army Form C. 2118.

WAR DIARY or **INTELLIGENCE SUMMARY**

135th Field Ambulance

Vol XI. Appx-1.

Place	Date	Hour	Summary of Events and Information	Remarks and references to Appendices
Camp 125	1916 May 1st		Arrangements for transfer of XIV Corps Rest Station from SAILLY LAURETTE to MARICOURT started – No further cases admitted from Corps Main Dressing Station from today –	
SAILLY LAURETTE MAP ALBERT 1/40,000 J.35.b.6.5.	2nd		Equipment being inspected (in Ambulance transport) & MARICOURT. Two men died down – Number of patients remaining 531 –	
	3rd		Men continued. Capt. W.R.P. McKNIGHT rejoined from special leave this afternoon and reported to C.M. D.S. MARICOURT –	
MARICOURT	5th		40th Gur. R.A.M.C. Operation order No. 25 dated 3.5.16 received (does not affect this unit) Headquarters of Ambulance moved to MARICOURT to take over XIV Corps Rest Duties from 26th Field Ambulance – A detachment of 2 officers and personnel remain at Camp 125 to evacuate patients remaining and set up equipment	
ALBERT 1/40,000 A.21.a.88			Detachment at XIV Corps Rest Station at CHIPILLY –	
	6th		XIV Corps Main Dressing Station taken over & now running as XV Corps Rest Station. 600 patients transferred	

SECRET

Army Form C. 2118.

135th Field Ambulance

WAR DIARY
or
INTELLIGENCE SUMMARY.
(Erase heading not required.)

VOL XII Page 2

Place	Date	Hour	Summary of Events and Information	Remarks and references to Appendices
	1917			
XV Corps Rest Station MARICOURT	May 8th		Evacuation & removal of equipment from old C.R.S - SAILLY LAURETTE to MARICOURT continued -	
ALBERT 40---	10th		All patients now cleared from SAILLY LAURETTE - 190 transferred to new C.R.S. Intimation received that No 75 D.31 PYH J COLLEY RAMC has been transferred to R.E.	
	11th		be transferred unit to Minute and is struck off strength of unit	
A 21.a.6.6	12th		Capt B. P. ALLINSON RAMC struck on sick list (General Debility)	
	13th		One tent subdivision of 136th Field Ambulance in charge of Capt. HEWITT RAMC departed to take over Officers Rest Station BUS DE L'ABBEY -	
			No M/2/105956 Pte F A LONGMAN-A.S.C. attached to this unit permission to drop & attend to O/2 GHQ Supply Column HESDIN E.F. (asked for Division for a temporary communion in A.S.C (Mechanical Transport)	
	14			
	16.40		Patients admitted 91 discharged to duty 13 transferred to P.O.S.? Remaining 57 less	
			17 O.R. 625	
	17.30		Capt - F. G. THATCHER RAMC struck of strength of unit on posting to D.A.D.M.S	
			40th Div	
			Capt J. M. MACKENZIE - RAMC (TC) posted to the unit	

2353 Wt. W2514/1454 700,000 5/15 D.D. & L. A.D.S.S./Forms/C. 2118.

SECRET

WAR DIARY
or
INTELLIGENCE SUMMARY
(Erase heading not required.)

Army Form C. 2118.

135th Field Ambulance

Vol XII Page 31

Place	Date	Hour	Summary of Events and Information	Remarks and references to Appendices
	1919			
MARICOURT	May 19th		Patients admitted 22 discharged to duty 23 & C.C.S. 3	
ALBERT	20th		No 24/13 Pte G. J. McLay RAMC was to-day transferred from 136 F.A. to this unit	
4070/9			Capt. B. P. ALLINSON RAMC taken off the sick list and resumed duty	
A.21			40th Sanitary RAMC attd No 24 Field Amb 20.5.19 returned (Have not before this unit)	
a 6.8.	21st		Two men duty transferred by No 4 Field Ambulance (Gunshot war site Fr VII 10/m Sedia Debim) Took over charge of Burial Ground off un Camp 2 4 E 4 R	
			Patients admitted 36 – discharged to duty 25 transfd to CCS6 Remaining 19 Officers – OR 632 –	
	22nd	–	No M/10927 Pte S. J. CONNOCHIE ASC MT was transferred to a CCS from 25th DSC and in charge of strangles of this unit from that date –	
	23rd		Capt S. E. McCLATCHEY RAMC (TC) joined & joined this unit to-day	
	25th		Capt BRENTNALL RAMC (T.F.) and one tent subdivision (20 O.R.) of 1st East Lancashire Field Ambulance arrived and on attached for duty to this unit	
	26th		Number of patients in the station – Admitted Officers 2 – O.R. 57 to duty Officers 1. OR 23	

WAR DIARY
INTELLIGENCE SUMMARY.

135th Field Ambulance Army Form C. 2118.

VOL XII Page 4

Place	Date	Hour	Summary of Events and Information	Remarks and references to Appendices
XV Corps Pre Station	1917 May 27		Evacuated to 41 St.H.P 8 – Nominum Offers 18 – Others ranks 670 – Admitted from Camp 125 on buses brought up for our Corps Sanitary Station	
MARICOURT			Attachment Field ambulance at Camp 125 lifting down tents	
ALBERT 40.000 A.21 a.8.8	28th		Nominum of horse transport from SAILLY-LAURETTE transferred to MARICOURT Coly. No. T/1/060550 Pte. J. GREEN A.S.C. admitted here own own by last part of a motor lorry while trying to alight under cover, he was admitted to No. 41 Stationary Hosp. Patients at Rest Station Admitted 63 to duty 14 – Officers admitted 3 – evacuated to 41 St.H.P B – Nominum Offers 20 – O.R. 691. Including 23 cases of scabies transferred from No. 5 C.C.S (closing down)	
	30th		Capt WESTLAKE R.A.M.C posted to this unit (in relief of Capt J. M. MACKENZIE R.A.M.C transferred to 50 Division) to be attached to 136 Field Amb for temporary duty.	
	31st		Patients at Rest Station – Admitted O.R. 45 – To duty 39 to C.C.S – 12 – Nominum Offices 21. O.R. 707. No. of embulants slightly wounded retained to duty after treatment 29 No. of convalescents sick treated & returned to duty 1.074 during month of May	

P/M Minut Lieut Col R.A.M.C
O.C 135th Field Ambulance

140/2230

No. 135. T. A.

June 1917

COMMITTEE FOR THE
MEDICAL HISTORY OF THE WAR
Date -7 AUG. 1917

Army Form C. 2118.

WAR DIARY
or
INTELLIGENCE SUMMARY.
(Erase heading not required.)

135ᵗʰ = Field Ambulance
Vol XII Page 1

Place	Date	Hour	Summary of Events and Information	Remarks and references to Appendices
III Corps Rest Station Halloy	1919 June 1st		Captain B.B. WESTLAKE R.A.M.C. doing temporary duty with 136 Field Ambulance	
HARICOURT ALIBERT 1 40.c.7.0	2nd		Proceeded to 4th Army School of Musketry for temporary duty. From No M/2/167760 Pte D.H. HOUGHTON A.S.C. M.T. received to A.C.C.S. to return to strength of unit	
A.21.a.8.8.	3rd		No 71741 a/Cpl H. BILSBOROUGH R.A.M.C. promoted a/Corporal from 30/4/19 D.G.M.S./B/1450/1848 dated 24/5/- XI Corps wired by III Corps today - Rest Station now known III Corps Rest Station. Two N.C.Os. proceeded to 40 Divn Gas School today for a three days course of instruction	
	4th		Patients in Rest Station - Admitted O.R. 24 To duty 36 To CCS 4 Remaining	
	5th		Officer in Station March 7/6	
	7th	10 am	Conducted of Rest Station Station continued No M/2/167760 Pte D.H. HOUGHTON - A.S.C. M.T. rejoined from No 4, 24 FA and is taken on strength of unit	
	8th		Arrangements made for transfer of convalescent cases requiring a further period of rest beyond curative art. to III Corps Convalescent Depot CERESY -	

WAR DIARY
or
INTELLIGENCE SUMMARY

Army Form C. 2118.

135th 2 Field Ambulance

Vol. VIII

Place	Date	Hour	Summary of Events and Information	Remarks and references to Appendices
Corps Rest Station	1917 June 9th		Patients in Rest Station – Admitted O.R. 63 – To duty 26. To C.C.S. 6 To Convalescent Depôt 29 – Nursing Officers 7 – Other ranks 739 –	
Rest Station	11th	11.40	Arrangements made for transfer of all cases from Station CHIPILLY to new Station MARICOURT adjoining Corps Rest Station	
MARICOURT				
ALBERT	13th	1.40	Patients in Rest Station. Admitted 29 – To duty 25. To C.C.S. 3. To Convalescent Depôt 47. Nursing Officers 8 O.R. 728 –	
4.175.77 21 a.6.8	14th		All cases from late Station CHIPILLY now transferred to MARICOURT. Personnel & equipment being brought up – Usual routine work at Corps Rest Station	
	16th	1.45	No. D.M./164396 A/Q.M. 72 Wilson A.S.C. M.T. granted pay for his acting rank from 16-9-16	
	19th	1.42	Nursing Staff – Admitted 41 – To duty 25 To C.C.S 10 To Convalescent Depôt 34 Nursing Officers 4 O.R. 808 –	
	21st		No 95921 Corp. W.C. WATERMAN – rank appointed a/Sergt without pay aut no. 71776 A/J/Q.M. J. RICHARDSON & No. 71732 A.J/Q.M. W.H. HARRISON appointed a/Corporals without pay to complete establishments	

Army Form C. 2118.

WAR DIARY
or
INTELLIGENCE SUMMARY.
(Erase heading not required.)

135th Field Ambulance

Vol XIII page 3

Place	Date	Hour	Summary of Events and Information	Remarks and references to Appendices
	1917			
III Corps	21st June		Nursing Staff Admitted 126. To duty 44. To C.C.S.6. To Convalescent Depot 33.	
Purr- Station	24th		Nursing 995 – Officers 2 – hand entire work of Purr Station	
MARICOURT	26th		Nursing 1075. Admitted 62. To duty 23. To CCS 8. To Convalescent Depot 16 –	
ALBERT			Nursing Officers 2. O.R. 486	
			III Corps Scabies Station now open at MARICOURT for reception of cases	
	28th		Nursing – No 41674 Pte F.P. McLEAN and No 41744 Pte J.J. WATSON	
A.21	29th		NAMC appointed acting hand orderlies with the Regt –	
a.8.8.	30th		No of patients returned to duty and to Convalescent Depot during month	
			Combatants sick. To duty 823	
			" " To Convalescent Depot 681	
			– do – slightly wounded To duty 24	
			" " To Convalescent Depot 10	

A.M. Wuut Lieut R.T. RAMC
oc 135th Field Ambulance

140/2298

No. 135. T. a.

COMMITTEE FOR THE
MEDICAL HISTORY OF THE WAR
Date 10 SEP. 1917

July 1917

Army Form C. 2118.

SECRET

WAR DIARY
or
INTELLIGENCE SUMMARY

(Erase heading not required.)

135th Field Ambulance
Vol XIV pages 1-

Vol 14

Place	Date	Hour	Summary of Events and Information	Remarks and references to Appendices
III Corps Rest Station	1917 July 1st		40th Divisional N.A.M.C. Order No 29 dated 30-6-17 received (not affecting this unit)	
MARICOURT	3rd		Order received from DDMS to attach three tent subdivisions of 136 Field Ambulance attached for duty to this unit in to begin headquarters of 136 F.A. on 6th inst	
ALBERT	4th		Capt. J. CRAWFORD M.C. R.A.M.C. proceeded to England on ten days leave. Medical arrangements III Corps received. Corps Rest Station MARICOURT is to close for further admissions after Sunday 8th inst. Rest Station to be handed over to an Ambulance of IV Corps at a date to be subsequently notified. III Corps Section Station about to be closed for admissions after 6th inst	
A.21 a 9.8.	6th		Achram sheets of 2 officers and 10 other ranks of 2/2 Home Counties Field Ambulance received	
			2/2 Home Counties F.A. Un in our section account for taking over	
	8th		Capt. B.P. ALLINSON R.A.M.C. admitting to 38 C.C.S. 40th Div D.A.M.C. Order No 30 received dated 6-7-17. To effect under Corps instructions 135th F.A. will hand over III Corps Rest Station MARICOURT to 2/2 H.C. Field Ambulance 58 Div - on July 9th & will then move to FINS	

WAR DIARY / INTELLIGENCE SUMMARY

135th Field Ambulance   VOL XIV Page 2

Place	Date	Hour	Summary of Events and Information	Remarks and references to Appendices
III Corps Rest Station MARICOURT	July 9th		and took over from 136th F.A. the evacuation of sick and wounded from the Left and Centre Brigades.	
	10th		Advance party with baggage proceeded to FINS. Handed over to Corps Rest Station with Details and all equipment - minimum changes to 2/2 Home Counties Field Ambulance - 40 Div RAMC of sick. 70 sgts 8 (7 sick) 135 Field Ambulance less one Officer and one Section O.R. (left at Maricourt) with 2/2 H.C. F.A.) proceeded to Fins.	
FINS France Sheet 57.c. V.12.c.6.7	11th		Took over Head Quarters Main Dressing Station FINS V.12.c.6.7 and Divisional Baths from 136th F.A.	
			Took over Advanced Dressing Station at Q.29.d.2.9 and Bearer Posts Q.30.b.05.9 R.19.b.11 - R.13.a.9.35 and R.2D.a.2.9. Left Brigade also Bearer posts at R.25.d.3.9 - R.26.d.5.05 - Centre Brigade	
	13th		Improved cellar use of small house at Q.36.d.6.9 GOUZEAUCOURT in view of construction of an alternate Advanced Dressing Station.	
	14th		Wound centrum - All wounded come back to Head quarters from A.D.S. Equipped to Divisional Main Dressing Station, with exception of Dear arms of Amulatory	

Army Form C. 2118.

SECRET

WAR DIARY
or
INTELLIGENCE SUMMARY.

(Erase heading not required.)

135 Field Ambulance   Vol XIV — page 3.

Place	Date	Hour	Summary of Events and Information	Remarks and references to Appendices
FINS	July 2	—	Wounds of head, thorax & abdomen and fracture of femur, which are evacuated direct to C.C.S. at YPRES	
Mep.	14th			
France	16th	—	19 O.R. reinforcements arrived from Base and on return on strength of unit	
S/C	18th	—	1 N.C.O. and 10 O.R. sent to GUIZANCOURT & employment at our A.D.S. in conjunction with R.E.	
Y.12.c.6.7	19th			
"	20th		Capt. J CRAWFORD 2nd H.C. rejoined unit on completion of tour of U.K.	
			Copy of Medical arrangements 4.0 Division recd from A.D.M.S.	
	21st		Capt. B.P. ALLINSON O.M.C. rejoined on discharge from 3# C.C.S.	
"	23rd		Arrived draft — 2 Bs. of patients and 10 O.R. reinforcing at Marquillies 4.0 F.Amb & 1st D.D.S.4	
	24th		War establishment at unit H.D.S. 90422.613.7 — at Fins — in front line renewed	
	26th		During night 25/26 gas shell bombardment of enemy with phos — phosgene	
			20 Green Round Through A.D.S. all slight into on evacuation	
"	27th		Capt. S.E. M'CATCHEY of this unit attached for temporary duty as M.O. to 1st & 15th Divl. regt.	
	29th		Capt. R. PROCTOR and 'C' Section of this unit required headquarters in continuation of temporary duty with 2/1 Home Counties Field Ambulance to supply part station	

Army Form C. 2118.

WAR DIARY
or
INTELLIGENCE SUMMARY.

(Erase heading not required.)

135th Field Ambulance

Place	Date	Hour	Summary of Events and Information	Remarks and references to Appendices
FINS DMS France	July 30th		One N.C.O. & 15 O.R. sent to new Divining Station GOUZEAUCOURT & await instructions. Lieut. G.W. WARD proceeded on leave to England.	
57-C V.12.C.S.7	31st		Usual routine. Preparation of war trainings and shelter at new Divining Station.	

J.R. Mont Lieut Col RAMC
OC 135 Field Ambulance

July 31st 1917

140/2364

No. 135. F.O.

Aug 1917

COMMITTEE FOR THE
MEDICAL HISTORY OF THE WAR
Date -1 OCT. 1917

SECRET   Army Form C. 2118.

135th Field Ambulance

WAR DIARY
or
INTELLIGENCE SUMMARY.
(Erase heading not required.)

Vol VI Page 1

Place	Date	Hour	Summary of Events and Information	Remarks and references to Appendices
FINS Map France August 57 c 1	1917 1st		D.M.S. 4th Army inspected Headquarters of unit	
	2nd		40th Division R.A.M.C. Order No 31 (Operation) received - to effect - In Corps Zone of Army extended Northern - Southern Boundary will be - Dc. L.9.7 - Q.S.d.9.7. Gouzeaucourt at Q.17.b.5.7. Neuman B GOUZEAUCOURT WOOD G.22.c.3.4 Gun Ravine K R.27.C.3.5. forming front boundary at K.28.d.5.5. — 135th F.A. (+ sufficient personnel from 137 F.A. will clear casualties from front held by 120th, 119th and left Bn. of 121st Infantry Brigades. F.A.D.S. at Q.29.d.2.9. Twelve O.R. sent from A.2. E.O/c. A.D.S. on horses for one Bearer Post at R.N.R. in rear front of line Bearer posts established at BEAUCAMP and CHARING CROSS 6 teams with 2 wheeled stretchers are each- evacuation into 4 A.D.S. arranged	
	3rd		Work at New A.D.S. - GOUZEAUCOURT - continued	
	4th		Work written	
	5th		Capt. W.J. ROBERTSON detailed for temporary duty in M.O. to 14th H.L.I.	
	6th		Capt. I.R. HUDLESTON R.A.M.C. posted to this unit Capt. R. PROCTOR. R.A.M.C. detailed for temporary duty at Divisional Main Dressing Station	

SECRET

Army Form C. 2118.

WAR DIARY
or
INTELLIGENCE SUMMARY

(Erase heading not required.)

135th Field Ambulance   Vol. IV Page 2.

Place	Date	Hour	Summary of Events and Information	Remarks and references to Appendices
F/NS	Aug 10"		Lieut. O.H. W. WARD rejoined on completion of leave to England	
M.D.S. Armee	12		Usual routine work on new A.D.S. and relay posts continued	
57.C			Capt. ROBERTSON rejoined on completion of duty with 145 M.H.Z.	
V.12.c.8.9	13"		Capt. BATHGATE R.A.M.C. M.O. 18th Bn has returned to Ambulance for temporary duty	
	16		Capt. HUDLESTON R.A.M.C. detached for temporary duty to D.A.D.M.S.	
	17"		Work on new Advanced Dressing Station continued – wired netting for operating	
			room fixed too – window unpacking pane – cement –	
	18"		Capt. W.J.D. ROBERTSON R.A.M.C. departed for England on expiration of contract and	
			in place of strength of unit	
	19"		Left Battalion left 13th mounted Hindquarters and R.A.P. from CHARING CROSS Q.17.B.2.8	
			& BEAUCHAMP O.18.b.8.9 – evacuation from two points now carried out via VILLERS	
			PLOUICH	
	21"		Bath Section at Hindquarters – Personnel 3.6 – Accommodat 14 – C.C.S. 1 – D.m D.S. 4 – duty 6	
			Personnel 3.9 – 40 Div. Name of Order No 32 duty 21½ used	
	23"		2 N.C.O. and 20 men attached for duty from 137 F.A. rejoined Their unit today	

WAR DIARY or INTELLIGENCE SUMMARY

Army Form C. 2118.

135th Field Ambulance

Vol. XV   page 3

Place	Date	Hour	Summary of Events and Information	Remarks and references to Appendices
FINS	1917 Aug 24th		Capt. B.P. ALLINSON R.A.M.C. placed on sick list.	
MAP	25th		Capt. B.B. WESTLAKE R.A.M.C. joined unit in connection of Sutpern emf X 4 – Army School of Musketry	
France 57.c			Capt WESTLAKE detached for temp. duty with 137 F.A. at Div. Main Dressing Station	
V.12.c.6.7	26th		Went unfitm State Numbering 41 – ommitted 15 – to C.C.S.1. D.M.D.S. 4 – only 6 numbers 45 –	
	27th		No. 71820 S/Sergt Price - No. 75047 Pte Tumelty rejoined on completion of course of 7th Army School of Cookery – ALBERT –	
	29th		Lieut R.K. MUSPRATT – R.A.M.C. posted to unit for duty	
	31st		Lieut P.K. MUSPRATT proceeded to report to O.C. 12th Yorkshire Regt as Officer in Med. Charge – and is struck off strength of this unit. No. of combatants attached to duty from Hindquarters Ambulance seven units 15-5 ORIGINAL	

M.M. Murr Lieut. C? Name
O.C. 135 Field Ambulance

No. 135. 7.a.

40/248

COMMITTEE FOR THE
MEDICAL HISTORY OF THE WAR
Date -5 NOV.1917

WAR DIARY
INTELLIGENCE SUMMARY

135th Field Ambulance

Vol XVI page 1

Vol 16

Army Form C. 2118.

Place	Date	Hour	Summary of Events and Information	Remarks and references to Appendices
France MAP FRANCE 57C V.12.C.6.9	1917 Sept 1st		Proton work as usual — Capt P J GAFFIKIN RAMC (SR) reported for duty from 136 F.A. and in turn in strength of unit — Capt. I R HUDLESTON RAMC proceeded for duty to 136 F.A. and is struck off strength of this unit —	
	3rd		7 rs. O.R. proceeded to THIRD ARMY Rest Camp VALERY-SUR-SOMME for change of air	
	4th		Capt B P ALLINSON took off sick but assumed duty. Capt WESTLAKE reported unit & proceeded to relieve Capt G.E. McCLATCHEY on M.D.E. 16th Welsh Regt.	
	6th		Capt McCLATCHEY proceeded to England on 14 days leave in receipt of ambulance — Medical arrangements 40th Divn dates 5-7-17 received from A.D.M.S	
	8th		Moved billets — 10 P.B. men arrived from Base (5 reported 10 A.S.C. Battalion (Coy 4) on taken on strength of unit — 10 A.S.C. Battalion detachment for Base and an extension of strength of unit —	
	10th		Rear Admiral Dewar Station at GOUZEAUCOURT completed and taken over in A.D.S. at Q.29.d.2.9. wounded (a blazing pair left in charge) — All casualties now evacuated through A.D.S. at GOUZEAUCOURT — Q.36.d.6.0. thence by Divisional railway and Motor Ambulances evac. to H.Q. FINS —	
	11th		Capt R PROCTOR RAMC reported unit on completion of temporary duty as M.O. 13th East Surrey Regt.	

WAR DIARY

INTELLIGENCE SUMMARY

135th Field Ambulance Vol XVI/Aug 2

(Erase heading not required.)

Army Form C. 2118.

Place	Date	Hour	Summary of Events and Information	Remarks and references to Appendices
FINS	1917 Sept 13th		Usual routine work — few casualties in front line D.M.S. 4th Army inspected our ADS at GOUZEAUCOURT —	
MAP FRANCE 57.C V.12.C.8.7	14th		26 Canadians passed through ADS route of reinforcements against enemy trenches	
	15th		Capt W.E. BATHGATE reported 15th Welsh Regt in connection of temporary duty with this unit	
	16th		Major TORREY and Major McKENN U.S. Medical Corps attached for temporary duty. Capt R. PROCTOR RAMC detailed for temp duty to M.O. 40th Div Engineers Lieut J.H. FISCUS M.O.R.C. USR present for duty with this unit.	
	17th		Usual routine — Arrangements for carrying out Funeral [illegible] for [illegible]	
	18th		Army being employed on Divisional Baths at GOUZEAUCOURT & FINS. Pte J. PHILLIPS 19th Welsh Regt died from G.S.W. abdomen at Main Dressing Station (Cleveland)	
			No 28027 Pte J PHILLIPS (Cleveland)	
"	21st		A raid on enemy trenches & ½ carried out 7pm tonight by 4th HLI. Our M.O. & 8 Bearers sent to reinforce Regt Med personnel [illegible] attached. Bearers sent to ADS as reinforcements	
"	22nd		No 76039 Pte W.H. LESTER RAMC reported unit from No 237 Dent Employment Co	

Army Form C. 2118.

WAR DIARY
or
~~INTELLIGENCE SUMMARY~~

135 7th Divisional

(Erase heading not required.)

Vol ??? page 3

Instructions regarding War Diaries and Intelligence Summaries are contained in F. S. Regs., Part II. and the Staff Manual respectively. Title pages will be prepared in manuscript.

Place	Date	Hour	Summary of Events and Information	Remarks and references to Appendices
FINS	Sept 23rd		Major H.M. TORREY & Maj. G.E. McLEAN - M.O.R.C. U.S. ARMY proceeded to No.55 C.C.S. on duty in completion of temporary duty with this unit	
MAP FRANCE 57.6	24th		No 9742 Pte H. CLARK 119 F. Amb. transferred to 38 C.C.S. on completion of C.S.M.	
	25th		Capt B B WATSON R.A.M.C. detached for temporary duty as M.O. 118 Bde R.F.A. ht.	
V.R. C.8.7	26th		Usual routine	
	27th		No 9 Camb Amb returned to duty. O.R. 80 (during month)	
	28th		Lieut Col. R.N. & Lieut. MANE referred on completion of ten days leave to England	
	30th		on 28-9-17	

B.M. Monk Lieut Col R.A.M.C.
OC 135 = Field Ambulance

40/2499

135th F.A.

6.1.17

COMMITTEE FOR THE
MEDICAL HISTORY OF THE WAR
Date -8 DEC. 1917

WAR DIARY
or
INTELLIGENCE SUMMARY

Army Form C. 2118.

135th Field Ambulance
VOL XVIII Page 1

Place	Date	Hour	Summary of Events and Information	Remarks and references to Appendices
FINS	1914 Oct 1st		Usual routine	
MAP	2nd		40 Div Order No 33 Name 2 F.A. ordered (to effect than 40th Division will be relieved by 20th Division between 1/6th – 7/6th October)	
France 57C			135th F.A. will be grouped with 120 & 2 Inf Bdes – 135 F.A. will be relieved by	
V.12-0-8.9	3rd		an ambulance of 20th Div proceeding on 6th inst. Ambulance to 40 Div Name Order No 33. "135 F.A. to complete handings over by 5 p.m. 6th inst	
	4th		Advance Party from 60th Field Ambulance 20th Division arrived – Capt J. CRAWFORD R.A.M.C. detailed for temporary duty in M.O. 19 R.W.F. M.M. Peronne – Outpatients attended to must depend on shifting in details of strength	
	5th		Advanced Dressing Station GOUZEAUCOURT – Became quota + relay posts and Brown Dummy Station FINS handed over to 60th Field Ambulance – Relief complete 5 p.m. –	
	6th		Ambulance proceeded by march route to PERONNE by march route and found 120 th Infantry Bde Group in billets – Capt S.E. McCLATCHEY R.A.M.C. reported on completion of leave –	
PERONNE	7th		In billets PERONNE – kit + clothing inspection etc.	

Army Form C. 2118.

WAR DIARY
or
INTELLIGENCE SUMMARY

(Erase heading not required.)

SECRET

135th Field Ambulance   Vol XVII   page 2.

Place	Date	Hour	Summary of Events and Information	Remarks and references to Appendices
PERONNE	Oct 1914 8th		CAPT. McCLATCHY. RAMC Tk on permanent medical charge of 19th R.W. Fusiliers and on strength off strength — CAPT. J. CRAWFORD detailed for temp duty on M.D. & 14 H.L.I.	
	9th		Sent two M.B. transport in 2 lieutenant & G.S. Waggons departed 7.20 a.m in charge of Capt McNeight RAMC in route for BERNEVILLE via BAPAUME —	
BERNEVILLE	10th		Ambulance less transport returned at PERONNE at 1 a.m. and arrival at BUSIFUX AU MONT at 11 a.m en route by motor route to Villers au BERNEVILLE arriving 1.30 a.m.	
I.O.C.S	11th		In billets during station for reception of sick from 120th B'h group estimated — working & Q immunied Buffer out BERNEVILLE & SIMONCOURT carried out & Ambulance	
I. 3	12th		O Denture — Physical training — Gas drill — First Aid instruction — Stretcher drill &c	
	14th		Capt B.B WESTLAKE rejoined on completion of temp duty with 11th K.O.R.L. Regt	
	15th		Capt. J. CRAWFORD RAMC proceeded on leave to England on account of contract	
	16th		Capt. B.P. ALLINSON detailed for temporary duty with 14 H.L.I. Usual routine + training	
	17th		No. 392263 Pte. T.M. FOX, RAMC died suddenly at 7.15 a.m from Cardiac syncope which set in after a short run — Court of Inquiry held —	
	18th		Usual routine	

Army Form C. 2118.

SECRET

WAR DIARY
or
INTELLIGENCE SUMMARY

135th Field Ambulance
Vol XVI Page 3

(Erase heading not required.)

Place	Date	Hour	Summary of Events and Information	Remarks and references to Appendices
BERNEVILLE	Oct 1916 20th		Under instructions from ADMS 40 Div Capt F.J. GAFFIKIN. R.A.M.C. reported for duty to O.C. 136th Field Ambulance and is struck off strength — Capt H. WARD-SMITH R.A.M.C. from 136th F.A. reported to this unit for duty and is taken on strength	
LENS	22nd		Capt R. PROCTOR held for permanent duty to 40 Div Engineers in relief off strength. Usual Routine — Much rain during night —	
I.3	23rd		Details off personnel + transport for internment funeral L Dev. B = head quarters	
	25th		Board continues —	
	27th		Instructions re Ommum Dustin received from 120th Inf Bde Gp	
	28		R.A.M.C. 40th Division Order No 34 dated 28/10 received 4 officers 40 Dragoon will march to LUCHEUX area on 29th inst — Field Ambulances will be personnel with Inmm Brigades or for last move. 120th Brigade Order No 138. 26.10.17 giving details of move received.	
	29th		Ambulance marched off with 120th Bde at 11:30 am arrived billets at GRENAS at 4:15 pm	
RENAS M.M.	30th		A. Willits arrangements made for carrying sick of Brigade Groups — also for 9 mm of Battn for troops in area at HALLOY —	
ENS				

Army Form C. 2118.

WAR DIARY
or
INTELLIGENCE SUMMARY

135th Field Ambulance

Vol — XVII page 4

(Erase heading not required.)

Place	Date	Hour	Summary of Events and Information	Remarks and references to Appendices
RENAS / LENS / 10000 F.15	1917 Oct 31st		Ambulance in billets with No B" Group — Sick evacuated to No 3 Canadian Stationary Hospital. DOULLENS —	

A.M.Hunt Lieut Col AMC
oc 135th Field Ambulance

140/2578

COMMITTEE FOR THE
MEDICAL HISTORY OF THE WAR
Date   17 JAN. 1918

No. 135. F. C.

SECRET

WAR DIARY
OR
INTELLIGENCE SUMMARY
(Erase heading not required.)

Army Form C. 2118.

135= Field Ambulance

VOL. XVIII Page 1

Place	Date	Hour	Summary of Events and Information	Remarks and references to Appendices
GRENAS	1917 Nov 1st		In billets GRENAS. Baths at HALLOY opened and worked by this Ambulance for personnel of 120th Bde Group - Capt M°NEIGHT - RAMC departed on one month special leave to England - Seven allotment granted to unit -	
MAP - 1/10,000 LENS	2nd		Arrangements made for Sanitary and Medical charge of 120th M.G Coy 2/120th T.M.B at WARLINCOURT - Capt. B.P. ALLINSON RAMC returned unit on completion of temporary duty with 14th H.L.I and proceeded to England on fourteen days leave -	
F.3	4th		In billets GRENAS. Physical training and instruction of personnel continued. Weather very wet	
	5th		One N.C.O + one orderly sent to III Corps Reinforcement Camp MONDICOURT for duty at Rest Inspection Room	
	7th		Usual routine - Weather - Still much rain	
	8th		A.D.M.S inspected billets of unit and baths at HALLOY - Capt J. CRAWFORD returned on completion of leave -	
	9th		Average number of men away on leave from unit. Ten daily. Still much rain.	
	10th		Lieut S.H. FISCUS M.O.R.C. U.S.A (attached to this unit) detailed to take on temporary Medical charge of 14th Argyle + Sutherland Highlanders	

Army Form C. 2118.

WAR DIARY
or
INTELLIGENCE SUMMARY

(Erase heading not required.)

135th Field Ambulance

Vol XXIV Page 2

Place	Date	Hour	Summary of Events and Information	Remarks and references to Appendices
GRENAS	Nov 1917 12th		In billets GRENAS - Work routine - Weather still wet	
MAP	14th		40th Div. D.A.M.C. Operation Order No 35 dated 14-11-17 received - To effect there 40 Div (Cdn Artillery) H.Q. R.E. 2½ Field Coy. R.E., 12th Yorks. Regt.) will move from LUCHEUX Area to FOSSEUX Area on November 16th. Field Ambulances will be grouped with same Brigades as for last move - Units will be occupy vacated billets in FOSSEUX Area.	
LENS 10A/BB10	15th		120th Bde. Order No 139 15/11/17 received - To effect 120th Inf. Bde. will march & billet in BERNEVILLE and SIMENCOURT on 16th November. -	
F.5.	16th		Ambulance left GRENAS at 10.3 a.m. and marched to BERNEVILLE, arrived 3.30 p.m. Billets for men & billets.	
BERNEVILLE	17th		120th Bde. Order No 140 17/11/17 received, to effect 120th Inf. Bde. Group will march from BERNEVILLE Area to COURCELLES-LE-COMTE on night of 17th/18th November. Information received from A.D.M.S. that all M.Os where leave was due to expire after 20 inst have been ordered to rejoin their units forthwith	
LENS 10A/BB10 T.3				
COURCELLES LE COMTE	18th		Ambulance left BERNEVILLE at 7.30 p.m. and arrived at COURCELLES at 12.45 a.m. 18/11/17. 120th Bde. Order No 141 18/11/12 to effect 120th Bde Group will move from COURCELLES-LE-COMTE to BEAULENCOURT on night of 18/19th November — 135/9A F.A. at starting point at 10.22 p.m.	

Army Form C. 2118.

WAR DIARY
or
INTELLIGENCE SUMMARY

(Erase heading not required.)

135th Field Ambulance.

Vol. XVIII Page 3

Place	Date	Hour	Summary of Events and Information	Remarks and references to Appendices
COURCELLES LE COMTE S7/c	1916 Nov 19th	4.30 p.m	Orders received from 120th Bde to effect that 135th F.A. will form Casualty point at 6.22 A.m. Ambulances left COURCELLES-LE-COMTE at 6.22 A.m and arrived in billets at BEAULENCOURT — LE	
TRANSLOY NORD S7/c 15 & 50		10.30 p.m	TRANSLOY NORD in 10 30 p.m Wire received from 120th Bde to effect that after 10 AM today all units of 40th Division will be ready to move at one hours notice.	
N 24 d. 6.4 S7/C Sheet 57C 40,000	20th	2.30 p.m	40th Division R.A.M.C Order No 37 dated 20/11 received to effect that 40th Division will move at one hour notice to BEAUMETZ-DOIGNIES area and will form Reserve in present position until further orders — 135th Field Ambulance will remain forward in present position until further orders — Motor transport of 3 F.A.s of Division will be pushed with 136th F.A. at BARASTRE and will come under orders of A.D.M.S. Check x x x.	
do	21st		Ammunition orders — in billets	
	22nd		Information received from A.D.M.S. that from 9 a.m 40 Division comes under administration of IV Corps. R.A.M.C. 40th Div Op Order No 38 received of IV Corps. R.A.M.C. 40th Div Op Order No 39 22/11 received — giving outline of intention & scheme for IV Corps front — R.A.M.C. Op Order No 40 22/11 received to effect that 40th Div will attack BOURLON WOOD — 119 Inf Bde will lead followed by 121st Inf Bde 120th Bde will be in reserve — 137th F.A will follow 119 Inf Bde and will be responsible for evacuation of casualties	

WAR DIARY
or
INTELLIGENCE SUMMARY

Army Form C. 2118.

135th Field Ambulance

Place	Date	Hour	Summary of Events and Information	Remarks and references to Appendices
N.24 d.6.4 57/1	Nov 22nd 1916		Firm Dismissed front x.x.x.x Advanced H Qrs of Div will open at HAVRINCOURT CHATEAU at 6 a.m tonight – New headquarters will open BEAUMETZ at 8 a.m and open at NEUVILLE-BOURJON Val at same hour – Capt WARD SMITH RAMC detailed for temporary duty with 136 F.A.	
"	23rd	7 a.m	Message received from A.D.M.S. "In confirmation of telegram from at once to TRESCAULT with all necessary personnel equipment and transport" (original telegram not received.) Ambulance left LE TRANSLOY at 8.30 a.m.	
"	"	11 a.m	Received message which on march at YTRES from A.D.M.S – Sent on M.O. to HAVRINCOURT at once. Capt J CRAWFORD despatched – also an order to send Bearer Division and his Tent subdivision at once to report at office of A.D.M.S HAVRINCOURT when they will be sent up to GRAINCOURT to reinforce 137th Field Ambulance – as many stretchers and dressings as possible should be carried – three officers should be sent	
TRESCAULT	24th	2 a.m	Arrived at TRESCAULT 2 a.m (Road traffic much congested) – Message received from ADMS "Find old arrivedible personnel to repair to this office at once". Employers of personnel transport – surgical haversacks – stall dressing haversacks as stretchers and personnel including all Medical Officers despatched to HAVRINCOURT – Blankets and stretchers	

Army Form C. 2118.

WAR DIARY or INTELLIGENCE SUMMARY

135th Field Ambulance
VOL XVIII Page 5

Place	Date	Hour	Summary of Events and Information	Remarks and references to Appendices
TRESCAULT	24th	—	Sent in Motor Ambulance cars. Personnel distributed by A.D.M.S. from HAVRINCOURT to report for duty to O.C. 137 F.A. at GRAINCOURT arrived at GRAINCOURT 6 a.m. and commenced distribution forming up under orders of O.C. 137 F.A.	
	25th		Headquarters — transport at TRESCAULT — Under instructions from A.D.M.S. made arrangements for carrying all wounded during trouble stretcher & medical comforts to Dump at HAVRINCOURT and from there by linestand 9.5 to GRAINCOURT — Horsed Ambulances supplement to 137th F.A. 40th Div. R.A.M.C. Order No. 42 25/11 issued to effect — 40 Div (less artillery 12 M.G. Coy. and 12th York Pioneers) will be relieved by 62nd Division to-night 25/26 inst. When relieved by F.A. of 62nd Div — R.A.M.C. personnel will withdraw as follows — 135 F.A. to F.A. Headquarters at TRESCAULT — 136 & 42nd 135 F.A. at TRESCAULT — 137 & 137 F.A. H.Q. at HERMIES — All vehicles withdrawing horsed Ambulances will form at 4.14 2nd 136 F.A. at TRESCAULT — All equipment in trim of motor lorries, also Table will be handed over to 62nd F.A. x x x	
	26th		Personnel of unit arrived at Headquarters at 8.30 a.m. — Convalescent ambulance by unit with attachment to 137 F.A. three wounded on R.S.M. shell shock and one sick	

Army Form C. 2118.

WAR DIARY
or
INTELLIGENCE SUMMARY.
(Erase heading not required.)

135th Field Ambulance
No. XVIII Page 6

Place	Date	Hour	Summary of Events and Information	Remarks and references to Appendices
TRESCAULT	March 26th		entrenched — Notification received of death from shell wounds of Pte ROBSON R.A.M.C wounded on 24th	
	27th	5 a.m.	Remainder of personnel who had been detached in Station train returned to camp —	
		9 a.m.	Wire received from O.9.m.8 instructing that unit should be prepared to entrain on short notice into 120th Inf Bde —	
		10.30	Personnel marched by march route to YTRES to entrain for BEAUMETZ RIVIERE	
		12.30	Transport joined transport column of 120th Bde & moved via BAPAUME	
		1 p.m.	Personnel arrived YTRES and entrained at 3.30 p.m. detrained BEAUMETZ 8.15 p.m. and marched to camp billets at BLAIRVILLE - HENDICOURT	
BLAIRVILLE	28th		In billets — Transport arrived in camp 3 p.m. Refitting and re-equipment commenced	
MAP. LENS II Squares I - 4	29th		Capt. WARD-SMITH R.A.M.C rejoined from 136 F.A. Capt. J. CRAWFORD - R.A.M.C transferred to No 3 Stationary Hosp - DOULLENS suffering from Neurasthenia. Brigade baths, foot-inspection, enemy order —	
	30th		In billets — Re equipment continued	

J.M. Munt Lieut Col R.A.M.C
O.C. 135 Field Ambulance

SECRET

Confidential

War Diary

of

135 Field Ambulance.

1st Dec 1917 to 31 Dec 1917.

(Volume XIX)

B Wilmot Lieut Col RAMC
OC 135th Field Ambulance

Army Form C. 2118.

WAR DIARY
or
INTELLIGENCE SUMMARY.

(Erase heading not required.)

135th Field Ambulance   VOL XIX   Page 1.

Place	Date	Hour	Summary of Events and Information	Remarks and references to Appendices
BLAIRVILLE	Dec 1917 1st		Signal message received from A.D.M.S. 2nd Br. proceed to same at 1.30 hours notice — Sent one officer and one imp. car to 136 F.A. at BEUVILLERS — Capt WESTLAKE dispatched	
MAP			40th Divn R.A.M.C Order No 44 dated 1-12-17 issued — To effect 40th Division will relieve	
LENS II 1/20,000			the 16th Division in the line x x x F.Ao will be prepared as far west as x x 135th F.A will relieve 113th F.A with Headquarters at SAPIGNIES on 3rd December x x x D.C. 135 F.A will attend an advance party of 1 officer and 10 O.R. to proceed to SAPIGNIES on 2nd inst	
I-4	2nd		Detach of 1 officer to arrange return Co Commanding Officer Proceeded with advance party to Headquarters 113 F.A. SAPIGNIES to arrange details — Suffered journey over by 6 digit instruction of Regt section being taken over from 16 Div to relieve personnel of 113 F.A at Advanced Dressing Station ECOUST C2.C.4.B (Sheet 57c) and at rear part at RAILWAY RESERVE 11.27.6.7.2 —	
SAPIGNIES	3rd		Ambulance left BLAIRVILLE at 9.45 a.m and proceeded to SAPIGNIES by march route arrived	
Sheet 57c		1.30 p.m.	Taking over of Ambulance Headquarters completed — 19 Patients handed over by 113 F.A	
1.6. 6-3-2	4th		Lieut Frano N.O.R.C. U.S.A. temporarily detailed for duty on M.D. and 2o McWilliam Reptd — Leave to England issued for personnel —	

2353 Wt. W2544/1454 700,000 5/15 D.D.& L. A.D.S.S./Forms/C. 2118.

Army Form C. 2118.

WAR DIARY
or
INTELLIGENCE SUMMARY.
(Erase heading not required.)

135th Field Ambulance

VOL XIX Page 2

Instructions regarding War Diaries and Intelligence Summaries are contained in F.S. Regs., Part II. and the Staff Manual respectively. Title pages will be prepared in manuscript.

Place	Date	Hour	Summary of Events and Information	Remarks and references to Appendices
SAPIGNIES H.8.b.3.2 (57.C)	1917 Dec 5		Ambulance at present serving Right Subsection of Right Section of 40th Div. Front - One RAMC Bearer Post and 1 Reg. Aid Post at Railway Reserve U.25.b.7.2. Personnel Gun Keenn - A.D.S. and Loading Post at ECOUST C.2.C.4.8. Personnel on M.C.S 4 Keenn - One Cmp. Ambulance Car to keep him Casualties evacuated to Main Dressing Station - SAPIGNIES H.8.b.3.2. Divisions in hospital. Headquarters 19 O.R.	
"	6		Capt. J CRAWFORD RAMC rejoined from No. 3 Canadian Stationary Hospital -	
"	7		Main Dressing Station Relieved - Personnel O.R. 47 E.C.C.S.9. duty 3.	
"	8		Capt. WARD SMITH - proceed to Sergennes on leave	
"	9		Capt. J CRAWFORD detached for temporary duty with 136th F.A. -	
"	10		1 caskn O.R. detached for temporary duty with No 20 C.C.S	
"	"	11.30 P.M	Message received from A.D.M.S. "Detail a large car & proceed at once and report to O.C 136 F.A. Gun Reserve Dinnum should be held in readiness to move at ½ an hour notice" Ipsissimum once -	
"	11th		Capt. H.M. POWELL RAMC joined to unit & taken on strength for record of sickness for duty with 137 F.A. -	
"	12th		An ambulance with Confederation from A.D.M.S. 23 O.R. of Braun Division posted to 135th F.A.	

WAR DIARY
INTELLIGENCE SUMMARY

Army Form C. 2118.

135 F.A. VOL XIX Page 3

Place	Date	Hour	Summary of Events and Information	Remarks and references to Appendices
SAPIGNIES	Dec 12th 1917	7 am	Sun enter from Smk to reinforce Beaver Park at RAILWAY RESERVE and no return on to ECOUST —	
H.Q. 6.3.2	12th	11.30 am	No of Autocar at Third Division — Minimum OR.77. Abnormal OR.22 to C.C.S. 0.2 OR.12 — In view of intention received of infantry attack on Divisional front in the morning, eight extra bearers sent to reinforce Bearer Posts with R.A.P. at Railway Reserve and Gas into farm to ECOUST —	
	13th		40th Div "NAME ORDER No 46" dated 13/12/17 to effect "In view of the temporary re-adjustment of VII Corps front the following moves of F.A.O. will take place. (a) 135 F.A. will move from SAPIGNIES on 14th December and take over F.A. duty at BOIRY BECQUERELLE from a F.A. of 34th Division × × × × from 15th December 135th F.A. will be responsible for the evacuation of casualties from the Left Subsection left system and will take over all posts etc from 135 F.A.: evacuation from A.D.S. HENIN POST being to H.Q: 136 F.A. HAMELINCOURT — 136 F.A. will take over the evacuation of casualties from the Right Subsection. Nipper station from 135 F.A. × × × A small hutting party will be left at ECOUST —	

WAR DIARY

INTELLIGENCE SUMMARY.

135th Field Ambulance

Vol XIX Page 4

Army Form C. 2118.

Place	Date	Hour	Summary of Events and Information	Remarks and references to Appendices
	1917 Dec			
SAPIGNIES	13		Further instructions received from A.D.M.S — "Send an advance party tomorrow morning to take over the F.A. site at BOIRY BECQUERELLE — The relief will be completed by 2 p.m. A holding party from an F.A. 25th Division will take over SAPIGNIES to-morrow morning."	
H.8.b.3.2				
BOIRY BECQUERELLE	14th		Arrangements for evacuation of Right section handed over to 136 F.A. - relief completed 12. noon — Advance party out to BOIRY BECQUERELLE. All patients evacuated to Corps Rest Station and C.C.S. and Ambulance sat at SAPIGNIES, marched on to holding party B.76 135 F.A. Ambulance marched to BOIRY BECQUERELLE and took over Ambulance Headquarters from 102nd F.A. 34th Div — Relief completed at 2 p.m.	
E.12.d.8.0 (51B)				
"	15th		Left section of left section taken over from 136th F.A. Relief completed at noon — Posts at R.A.P. and R.A.M.C. Berun Post at T.6.d.5.9 — Personnel 1 N.C.O. 12 tamm — R.A.M.C. Berun Relay Post. T.6.a.4.4 Personnel 6 tamm — Relay Post in Pill Box [illegible] T.5.a.5.2 personnel 8 tamm, Advanced Dressing Station and Loading Point HENIN POST T.2.b.7.7 personnel 1 N.C.O. 2 tamm. Two ambulance cars — Evacuation arranged to Head Quarters	

WAR DIARY or INTELLIGENCE SUMMARY

Army Form C. 2118.

136th Field Ambulance
Vol XIX Pag 5

(5)

Place	Date	Hour	Summary of Events and Information	Remarks and references to Appendices
BOIRY BECQUERELLE G·12 b·8·0 (51 B)	15		BOIREY from then Warrant t CCS BOISLEUX AU MONT – Sick t main Dressing Station 136 F.A. HAMELINCOURT – Stipulation received from A.D.M.S. t effect that when necessary Ambulance Trains will be sent up t C.C.S. at Avrelle Ste Legre and HENIN t transmit wounded direct t CCS (Duisans Duisans) leaving point for Ambulance Train (Duisans) estimated at T.2 b·14·4 – about 100 yds from A.D.S. – 15 O.R. (Seven) reported from temporary duty with 136 F.A.	
	16		Greater number of personnel proceeding on leave. Three for main – Total admission last 24 hours 4 O.R. General Shell Gas 2 – all cases transferred to 136 F.A Main Dressing Station or CCS –	
	17		Annual return Diary for admission form main L.D.M.C ANWARD forwarded t England on leave –	
	18th		Information received from Sir Hugh Jeadlaw – That the following N.C.O. + men had been awarded the Military Medal by IV Corps Commander – Ro.37/655 Corpl W·H·FOLEY· Ro.71815 Sjt W·C·E·FRANCIS·– Ro.75096 Pte J·H·HOLDSWORTH – Ro.76127 Pte W·R·HOLDEN – Ro.75030 Pte J· NEWMAN – Ro.71906 Pte J·COWAN – and No.74/057270 Gnr. S·DONALD· A.S.C. attached – for Gallant Conduct at BOURLON WOOD on 23rd 24th + 25th November 1917	
	20th			

T2134. Wt. W708—776. 500000. 4/15. Sir J.C. & 8.

WAR DIARY or INTELLIGENCE SUMMARY

Army Form C. 2118.

135th Field Ambulance
VOL XIX Page-6

Place	Date	Hour	Summary of Events and Information	Remarks and references to Appendices
BOIRY			Note in Divisional Orders re RAMC bearers "No stretcher bearers have performed their	
ECLUSELLE B.12.b.8.0 (51 B)			duties and dangerous duty in a more exemplary manner – They had specially to pass through enemy barrage fire and shrapnel whilst discharged for danger" u.O.S.C Dunn "Drivers Donald and Gumigan were each in charge of a horsed ambulance wagon – They showed utter disregard for danger – Although the shell in the village where the Advanced Dressing Station was situated was under continued fire they carried out their duties in a most praiseworthy manner and set a fine example to their comrades –	
	21"		40th Div Order No 115 20/12 received to effect at the Corps Front is in future to be held by two divisions – even with 121st Div in the front + + + on the Corps right in alongs + + on 24th inst the 121st Div + + on the left section of the front now held by the 3rd Div + + on the 29th the 120 + 13th will relieve the Right Section of the front now held by the 3rd Division	
	22"		Medal ribbons presented by G.O.C. III Corps to own awarded holding medal	

WAR DIARY

135th Field Ambulance

Vol. XIX Page 4

Place	Date	Hour	Summary of Events and Information	Remarks and references to Appendices
BOIRY BECQUERELLE S.12.6.8.0 (51 B)	Dec 1917 24th		40th Division R.A.M.C. Order No 47 dated 24/12/17 received — to effect re-adjustment of VI Corps Front — the filling over of F.A.s will take place on the 27th inst. 135 F.A. will hand over the A.D.S. and Bearer Posts of the Left Section, left system, to a F.A. of 34th Div — they will move from BOIRY BECQUERELLE to Field Ambulance area at BEHAGNIES. 135 Field Ambulance will take over from a F.A. of the 3rd Division the A.D.S. and Bearer Posts at ECOUST, and to rearrange for the evacuation of cases from the present Left Section of 3rd Division area, is being relieved by the 121st Bde — Move to be complete by 2 p.m. ＋ ＋ ＋ On 29th inst 135 F.A. will take over A.D.S. and Bearer Posts on the Right Section of the 3rd Divisional Front when is being relieved by the 120th B.M. — Inphiled A.D.S. of Right Section 3rd Div. Front with A.P.M.S. Capt. J.C. CRAWFORD — R.A.M.C. regarded after Inspection duties with 136 F.A. Capt. WARD-SMITH — R.A.M.C. regarded from leave	

WAR DIARY or INTELLIGENCE SUMMARY

Army Form C. 2118.

135th Field Ambulance
VOL XIX Page 8

Place	Date	Hour	Summary of Events and Information	Remarks and references to Appendices
BOIRY BECQUERELLE S.12.b.8.0 (51 B)	1917 Dec 25th		"Christmas Day - Arranged with O.C. 102 F.A. for handing over A.D.S. Headquarters site etc. of left section - left section front 40 D. in front. Officers out to men preliminary arrangements for taking over - H.D.S.s #3 at Dr front - Visited Headquarters of Y.m. & 8th & Y.ths 3rd Division	
	26th		Two M.O.s and 40 O.R. proceeded to ECOUST and took over A.D.S. and Beam Posts from No 7 Field Amb. 3rd Division and made arrangements for clearing sick and wounded from outer belts of new 40th Divisional Front	
	27th		Headquarters of Ambulance moved from BOIRY BECQUERELLE and took over F.A. site from No. 8 F.A. at BEHAGNIES	
BEHAGNIES 42.a.5.1 (57 C)	28th		Capt ALLINSON R.A.M.C. detailed for temporary duty with 17th Welsh Regt	
	29th		Capt CRAWFORD R.A.M.C. proceeded to V/4/1LX with 3.5 O.R. and 35 additional bearers from 137th F.A. and took over A.D.S. and Beam Posts from 8th F.A. 3rd Division and made arrangements for clearing sick and wounded from the Right Sector 40th Divisional new front	
	30th		Visited Advanced Dressing Station etc in own element by unit - all arrangements working satisfactorily	

Army Form C. 2118.

135th Field Ambulance
VOL XIX Page 9.

WAR DIARY
or
INTELLIGENCE SUMMARY.
(Erase heading not required.)

Place	Date	Hour	Summary of Events and Information	Remarks and references to Appendices
BEHAGNIES H2.a.5.1 (57C)	1917 Dec 31st		Headquarters and Horse Transport at BEHAGNIES. Tented personnel 69 - at Advanced Dressing Station ECOUST and VAULX and nearer Bivon Posts - Personnel 129 including 36 Bearers from 137 F.A. On leave 53 — at 2/3 C.C.S. 14 —	

A M Moore Lieut Col. N.Z.M.C
OC 135 Field Ambulance

No. 135. T.C.

COMMITTEE FOR THE
MEDICAL HISTORY &c.
Date -4 MAR. 1918

SECRET

Army Form C.2118.

WAR DIARY
or
INTELLIGENCE SUMMARY.

135th Field Ambulance.

Vol XX Page 1

(Erase heading not required.)

Place	Date	Hour	Summary of Events and Information	Remarks and references to Appendices
BEHAGNIES (H.2.a.5-1 57c)	1918 Jan 1st		Headquarters of Ambulance at Behagnies – Ambulances with reinforcement of 3 R. bearers from 137th F.A. during Night. Conter and part of left section of 40 Div Train BULLECOURT – Thro' Brigade in the line – Advanced Dressing Station for Night Posts. 120th Bde situated at VAULX C.20 d 2 8 – with two bearer relays – been collecting posts. Advanced Dressing Station for Centre & Right subsection of left section situated at ECOUST (119th – 121st Bde) C.2.c.4.8 with two bearer posts and two relay posts – Sick and wounded evacuated from VAULX by ambulance Decuaville train – Wounded direct to C.C.S. ACHIET LE GRAND – Sick & intermediary from ERVILLERS–BAPAUME Road thence by ambulance cars or hand ambulance wagon to 136 F.A. at HAMELINCOURT or 137 F.A. ERVILLERS	
"	3rd		Sick and Wounded from ECOUST direct by Motor Ambulance to C.C.S. or Field Ambulance	Nil
"	4th		Usual routine – normal condition – front line – Lieut. D. W. AWARD rejoins from leave – Lieut. Attwaters & men, hrs dong. Division O.R of unit reformed on completion of temporary duty at 20th C.C.S	Nil Nil

T2134. Wt. W708—776. 500000. 4/16. Sir J. C. & S.

SECRET

WAR DIARY
or
INTELLIGENCE SUMMARY

135th Field Ambulance
Vol XV Page 2

Army Form 2118

(2)

Place	Date	Hour	Summary of Events and Information	Remarks and references to Appendices
BEHAGNIES H.Q. A.S.I. (54 C.)	1918 Jan 6th		Arrangements made for a regular train service of Decauville Hospital Trams from VRAUX & ACHIET LE GRAND — Train to pick up cases at least evening at ECOUST A.D. brought down by ambulance cars from A.D.S. ECOUST	MW
	8th		Heard lecture at HENDECOURT on Construction & stable entrainment — Methods of inspection in front line — beyond own heavy shelling round A.D.S. VAULX in connection & examined Stables NOREUIL to find suitable accommodation for Cnts Tunnel Foot Assessment Centre for Right B'de Western still cold & frosty	MW
	9th			MW
	10th		Capt B.R. ALLINSON reported from temp duty with 17th Divn Rest Camp returned by Capt WARD-SMITH RAMC	MW
	11th		Two Motor Ambulance Cars attached from 30 M.A.C. for temporary duty — Change in weather — thaw commenced —	MW
	13th		Under instructions from G.O.M.S. Arrangements made for present change of level Corps 7.4 - 7 pm without M.O. — Capt Allinson joined in with him	MW
	14th		heard instruction from D.M.S. Army. 1st Lieut J.H. FISCUS U.S.M.R.C. attached to this unit is posted to 161 Tunnelling Company R.E. in charge of Hospital Weather Wet continues alternating with sharp frosts — emergent condition of horse & foot	MW

SECRET

Army Form C. 2118.

WAR DIARY
or
INTELLIGENCE SUMMARY.

(Erase heading not required.)

135th Field Ambulance
Vol VI Page 3

Place	Date	Hour	Summary of Events and Information	Remarks and references to Appendices
BEHAGNIES d 2 a 5-1 (57 C)	1918 Jan 17th		Capt A J BEVERIDGE - M.C. RAMC (from 137 F.A.) reported for duty and is taken on strength - Much rain - Trenches impassable owing to siden flaking in & fell through in many places	MMA
	18th		Trench foot cases occurring in small numbers - Anti-Trench foot Treatment Centre at ECOUST in working order - In every case drug cot on trenches has forth - obtained - Little activity in front line owing to weather conditions	MMA
	19th		Sun rain snow changing wind - trench condition still bad - A.D.S. VAULX again shelled own damage to trenches no casualties -	MMA
	20th		Trench warfare. Trench foot cases still occurring - Duties being fort Trenches Carts at NOREUIL nearly completed	MMA
	22nd		Little activity in front line owing to condition of ground. Weather mild no rain -	MMA
	23rd		Wind northerly -	MMA
	24th		Trench foot preventive fort Baths started working at NOREUIL - O.O. S ECOUST shelled this morning - No Casualties & personnel - Weather continues mild - trench condition improved -	MMA

(4)

SECRET

Army Form C.2118.

WAR DIARY
or
INTELLIGENCE SUMMARY.

135th Field Ambulance
Vol XX Page 4

(Erase heading not required.)

Instructions regarding War Diaries and Intelligence Summaries are contained in F. S. Regs., Part II. and the Staff Manual respectively. Title pages will be prepared in manuscript.

Place	Date	Hour	Summary of Events and Information	Remarks and references to Appendices
EHAGNES	1918 Jan 25th		Usual routine – Stables and other construction work continued at headquarters. Weather mild + dry – Trench condition improving – very fair "trench feet" cases	QMM
(2 a 5.1)	26th		Nothing of importance to record	QMM
(5 9 C)	26th		Little activity on front line. A.D.S. scout again shelled – Our own arnmgt [arrangement] hemmit [?] shelled from 137 ZIA "8 round" from enemy two shells at no 1 Relay Post	QMM
	29th		Usual routine – Clear moonlight nights – Intense bombing from enemy aircraft – in billeting area third time – during night – no casualties in unit – Work on protection with sandbag walls around huts at headquarters continued	QMM
	30th		Took A.S.M. 8.59th Division round Advanced Dressing Station at Corps Rest Camp GOUY. Bombing again during night near headquarters no casualties – Visited [?]	QMM
	31st		Usual routine – Work at headquarters continues – No bombing during night Weather cold & foggy	QMM

A M Monk Lieut Col RAMC
OC 135th Field Ambulance

140/2754

No. 135. T. A.

COMMITTEE FOR THE
MEDICAL HISTORY OF THE W...
Date -8 APR 1918

WAR DIARY or INTELLIGENCE SUMMARY

Army Form C.2

135th Field Ambulance
Vol XXI Page 1

Vol 21

Place	Date	Hour	Summary of Events and Information	Remarks and references to Appendices
BEHAGNIES H.2.a.5.1 57 C	1916 1st		Headquarters at BEHAGNIES – Front still during 40th Divisional front – A good deal of enemy artillery activity in front line – A Bty of 13th York Regt was shelled this morning while waiting for anti-tank fort treatment at Achiery Perm. ECOUST – (4 killed 19 wounded) – Anti tank fort treatment centre at NOREUIL also shelled (no casualties) Weather damp and foggy – No fighting last night. MMM	
	2nd		Anti tank fort treatment Centre at ECOUST Temporarily closed by order of D.in Headquarters owing to shelling – Damp and foggy – No bombing – MMM	
	3rd		Usual routine. On 7 Oct. sick and wounded from line still small – Clear night. Enemy aircraft seen again a man bomb dropped last night – No cases of trench foot in Division for some days – MMM	
	5th		Lieut. D. Mants A.M. WARD wounded to 47 C.C.S. MMM	
	7th		Usual routine. Protection work round huts & dugouts nearly completed MMM Visited III Corps Rest Station – Preparing to taking over from 103rd F.A.	
	8th		Sixty SIOS and McALLON – US MED CORPS attached to Ambulance for duty –	

WAR DIARY or INTELLIGENCE SUMMARY

Army Form C.

135 Field Ambulance — Vol XII

Place	Date	Hour	Summary of Events and Information	Remarks and references to Appendices
DEHAGNES H2.a5.1 (57C)	9/16 Feb 8th		40 Div name order no 49 dated 7/2/16 recund — 2 Officer 40th Div (Lieut. Quilley and Pricien will be relieved in the line by 59th Div (Lieut. Cuthillen) on 10th 11th 12th Feb — 135 F.A. will be relieved by the 2/1 North Midland F.A. on 11th inst — and on completion will move to YORK CAMP MERIATEL for the night 11/12th February — x x x — On the 12th inst 135 F.A. will move from MERCATEL to GOUY-EN-ARTOIS and will take over the VI Corps Rest Station GOUY, and Officers Rest Station BARLY from a Field Amb of 31st Division. An advance party of an Officer & 50. O.R. will be detailed to proceed to GOUY on the 8th inst + + + + + + + Capt ALLINSON and advance party proceded to GOUY this morning Lieut McMALLON — USAC proceded to ADS in chg of Capt BEVERIDGE RAMC	
	9th		who rejoined headquarters — Capt BEVERIDGE RAMC and further personnel proceded to VI Corps Rest Station GOUY to arrange detail of taking over	
	10th		Two Officers and similar O.R. of 2/1 North Midland Field Ambulance procedeed to advance Dressing Station at ECOUST & VAULX to arrange details of relief	

WAR DIARY or INTELLIGENCE SUMMARY

Army Form C. 2118

135th Field Ambulance

Vol XXI Page 3

Place	Date	Hour	Summary of Events and Information	Remarks and references to Appendices
BEHAGNES H2.a.5.1 (57 C)	1916 10th 11th		7/15 O.R. 2/1 N Midland F.A. proceeded to ECOUST, VAULX & relieve this unit. Redeployment of F.A. at Behagnes handed over to 2/1 N.M Field Ambulance. Relief at Advanced Dressing Station, Bearer Posts & in Dugout & Centre Subs completed at 5 a.m. Ambulance proceeded to billets at YORK CAMP MERCATEL — VII Corps Rest Station 9045 taken over from 103rd Field Amb	
	12th		by Acheux Park at 8 a.m. — 4/15 Palmer transferred 14 F.A. and remainder of Amt proceeded by cars and lorries march to VI Corps Rest Station from Camp Mercatel — (Officers Rest Station at B+R+F) taken over by CAPT ALLINSON from 103rd F.A on morning of 10th inst.	MMK MM
GOUY EN ARTOIS (51 C)	13th		Ambulance running — VII Corps Rest Station & VII Corps Officers Rest Station	MMM
	14th		Routine work arranged— Improvements & alterations carried on in Camp	MMM
GOUY EN ARTOIS (51 C)	15th		Lieut-Colonel R.N. Hunt DSO proceeded on leave routine work no the of further interest to report OPS	
	16th		A course of lectures for Medical Officers and Sergts on Camp started under arrangements by ADMS Corps First Aid to defense	

Army Form C. 2118.

WAR DIARY
or
INTELLIGENCE SUMMARY.
(Erase heading not required.)

Instructions regarding War Diaries and Intelligence Summaries are contained in F. S. Regs., Part II. and the Staff Manual respectively. Title pages will be prepared in manuscript.

Place	Date	Hour	Summary of Events and Information	Remarks and references to Appendices
GOUY-en- ARTOIS (51C)	Feb 16		by A.D.O.S. 6th Corps on Ambulance Q.B	
"	Feb 18		Accommodation of Rest Station being overloaded by heavy Sickness. In future the admissions are to be limited to 40 per day and instructions issued by D.D.M.S. 6th Corps to Divisions Q.S	
"	Feb 20th		Inspected by D.D.M.S. 6th Corps, very cordial but expressed dissatisfaction at the running of the Rest Station Q.S 1st Lieut C. Sine M.O.R.C. transferred to 7 th Army Medical School Q.	
"	Feb 22		Routine Work. Instructions received from Corps as to Divisional disposal of Sick in the event of a withdrawal Movements Q.S	
"	Feb 23rd 9 A		1st Lieut O. La Rotunda M.O.R.C. temporary attached from 13 & Field Ambulance. 1st Lieut R.F. McAloon M.O.R.C. detailed as Medical Officer to	

T2134. Wt. W708—776. 500000. 4/15. Sch J. C. & S.

Army Form C.2118

WAR DIARY
or
INTELLIGENCE SUMMARY.
(Erase heading not required.)

Instructions regarding War Diaries and Intelligence Summaries are contained in F.S. Regs., Part II. and the Staff Manual respectively. Title pages will be prepared in manuscript.

Place	Date	Hour	Summary of Events and Information	Remarks and references to Appendices
GOUY. EN ARTOIS (51C)	Feb 23		11th and 49th Squadrons Royal Flying Corps and Railway Operating Department at GOMBERMETZ. a/3	
"	Feb 24		6th Corps Commander (Lieut-General Sir A. HALDANE KCB DSO) inspected the Rest Station and Officers Rest Station expressing satisfaction at their organisation a/3	
"	Feb 27		40th Division R.A.M.C. order No 52 Copy no 10 received. 135 Field Ambulance responsible for Collection and treatment of Sick of 119 Brigade (infantry) 120 th Infantry Brigade order no 172 Copy no 18 Received Division move into G.H.Q. Reserve a/3	
"	Feb 28th		119th Infantry Brigade order no 154 received. Specific units for Entraining in the event of a move a/3	

Arthur J. Bennett
Capt R.A.M.C.
O.C. 135 Field Ambulance
28/2/18

140/2700.

135th Field Ambulance.

Dec. 1917.

COMMITTEE FOR THE
MEDICAL HISTORY OF THE WAR.
Date 6 JUN 1918

Army Form C. 2118.

WAR DIARY
or
INTELLIGENCE SUMMARY.

(Erase heading not required.)

SECRET

135 - 1st Field Ambulance.

Vol XXII Part 1

Vol 22

Instructions regarding War Diaries and Intelligence Summaries are contained in F.S. Regs., Part II. and the Staff Manual respectively. Title pages will be prepared in manuscript.

Place	Date	Hour	Summary of Events and Information	Remarks and references to Appendices
GOUY-EN-ARTOIS (51c)	1st March		Nothing of interest to report. G/3	
"	2nd March		Inspection by Acting A.D.M.S. (Lieut Colonel Huddlestone R.A.M.C.) Who gave verbal instructions regarding a relief of the Corps Rest Station by an Ambulance. 1st Lieut C. Sims M.O.R.C. Proceeded to No 3 Wing Balloon Section R.F.C. for Permanent duty as M.O. 3 copy no. 10	
"	3rd March	2 P.M.	40th Division R.A.M.C. Order no 53 D 2/3/18 received (64 Corps Rest Station to be taken over by an Ambulance of 34th Division on 4 inst. 135 Field Ambulance to move into Billets at BIENVILLERS (see 11, 177,000 H.4.D. Order for 135 Field Ambulance drafted accordingly) G/3	
"	"	5 P.M.	Advance party from 102 Field Ambulance (2 Officers 55 Other Ranks) arriving of this party and Officers and Q.R. went to Officers Rest Station at BARLY Rest of which men confided at 7 P.M. G/3	
"	4th	12 noon	Relief of 64th Corps Rest Station completed. Marched out at 2.P.M. to billets at BIENVILLERS G/3	
BIENVILLERS	4th	4 P.M.	Arrived at BIENVILLERS and BIENVILLERS. Lieut Colonel R.N.HUNT DSO RAMC Rel. BERLES-AU-BOIS and BIENVILLERS. Received instructions to take over the BERLES-AU-BOIS from last name proceeded to Divisional Headquarters on acting A.D.M.S. G/3	

SECRET

WAR DIARY
or
INTELLIGENCE SUMMARY.

Army Form C. 2118.

135 Field Ambulance
Vol XXII Page 2

Place	Date	Hour	Summary of Events and Information	Remarks and references to Appendices
BIENVILLERS Sheet 11 1/40,000 H.4.	March 5th		Baths at BERLES-AU-BOIS and BIENVILLERS open and in working order. Rechecking equipment. Capt Rutherford M.C. R.A.M.C. posted as Medical Officer I/c 40th Div Machine Gun Battalion. q.3.	
"	March 6th		Capt S.E. McKelly proceeded to temporary duty as M.O. I/c 21st Middlesex Regt. 120th (Highland) Infantry Brigade order no 174 Copy no 15 Received. (Detail of march routes and Entraining Stations in the country of a move) q.3.	
"	March 7th		6th Copy medical defence scheme received. In the event of an enemy action taking place the Motor Ambulances of the 40th Division would be pooled under ADMS 40th Div. and used for evacuating sick and lightly wounded from M.D.S's to CCS at GOUY-en-ARTOIS q.3.	
"	March 8th		Authority granted for the following promotions to be made in accordance with G.R.O. no 3448 dated Feb 23-2-18. 384 Captain A.J. Berridge R.A.M.C. S.R. to be O.C. (Major) and Lieut J S [?] CAS Sect III (4) and T/Captain	

SECRET

135th Field Ambulance

WAR DIARY
or
INTELLIGENCE SUMMARY.
(Erase heading not required.)

Vol XXII Page 3

Army Form C. 2118.

Place	Date	Hour	Summary of Events and Information	Remarks and references to Appendices
BIENVILLER Sh 11 100 000 H 4.5	March 8th		WRP McNight RAMC to be Actg Major Authority C.DS. 384 Sec VII (6)	
	March 10th		Capt J Crawford M.C. Transferred to 136 Field Ambulance. 1 Field O.P. Returned MORC Letter on attached. Amendment No 1 to 6th Corps Medical defence scheme Received. 120 Infantry Brigade Instruction No 1 Copy 13 D/10.3.18 received giving assembly points in the event of an enemy attack. 135 Field Ambulance grouped with 120 Infantry Brigade for this purpose. JB	9/3
	March 11th		40th Division RAMC Order No 555 D 11/3/18 Copy No 10 received. Division moves to BOISLEUX area on the night of the 12th to meet probable enemy attack on a 13 mile front. Low RAMC personnel to be moved in accordance with RAMC order No 54 D 8/3/18. JB 120 Brigade Order No 175 D 11.3.18 Copy No 11 received. 135 Field Ambulance to leave BIENVILLERS at 6.30 P.m. 12.3.18 and move to HAMELINCOURT Surplus kit to be dumped. One section equipment dumped in addition or instructions received from ADMS. JB	
	March 12th		Advance billets parties sent on to HAMELINCOURT in the morning	

Army Form C. 2118.

135th Field Ambulance
VOL XXII Page 4

SECRET
WAR DIARY
or
INTELLIGENCE SUMMARY.
(Erase heading not required.)

Place	Date	Hour	Summary of Events and Information	Remarks and references to Appendices
BIENVILLERS (Long H 1/40,000 H 4.5)	March 12th	P.m. 6.35	Left BIENVILLERS march in rear of 2.31 Field Amby R.E.	
HAMELINCOURT 51B (1/40,000) S 23.C.3.B.	March 12th	P.m. 10.50	Arrived at HAMELINCOURT MAP 51B 1/40000 S 23.C.3.B. (Army 1 Conf.) 9/- We 6th Corps front. Instructions received from A.D.M.S. that in the event of the infantry brigade moving forward one medical officer per Brigade and 12 O.R. per battalion would be attached thereto	
"	March 14th 16th		Notices of interest to report. Routine work and training 9/5	
	16"		Lieut Col R.N. Hunt assumed command of Ambulance on completion of European duty as A.D.M.S. 40th Division	MH
	17"		In Camp Hamelincourt guarded with 120th Bn. — Lieut McALDON + Dr ROTUNDA forwarded for a court of enlistment & W Cosh 1rd Lieut —— MH No 53971 Pte H NEWBERY RAMC tried by F. Gen. Court Martial at BLAIRVILLE on Charge "Stealing money the property of a Comrade" MH	
	19th		Warning Order from ADMS 40th Div to effect 40 Div will relieve 3 Div in Left Sect of VI Corps Front between 22nd + 24th March. 135 F.A. will relieve the Divisional	

Army Form C. 2118.

Instructions regarding War Diaries and Intelligence Summaries are contained in F. S. Regs., Part II. and the Staff Manual respectively. Title pages will be prepared in manuscript.

SECRET

WAR DIARY
or
INTELLIGENCE SUMMARY.

(Erase heading not required.)

135th Field Ambulance
Vol XXII Page 5

Place	Date	Hour	Summary of Events and Information	Remarks and references to Appendices
HAMILINCOURT CAMP I.B 4000 S.23.c.3.8. RHAGH	20" 21" 22"		Main Dining Station at the Brickfields S.2.b.7.4 - 136.7A vd clue on Right Bn Frnt - 137.7A vd clue Lift Bn Frnt MM# Ambulance at Armagh Camp — MM# Heavy bombardment of W Corps front by enemy early this evening followed by Infantry Attack — Penetration of Snd lines of 7.9 Contonwood on No 53971 Pvt H. NEWBERRY R.A.M.C. carried out on parade — Sentence 9 months imprisonment with hard Labour — to be put under 2t/M/year until sentence is confirmed — Put it to committed to prison at Frevent — 12.0 pm 5th Inf Bn proceeded from HAMILINCOURT to reinforce 59th Division — Been Subaltern under command of Maj. BEVERIDGE — R.A.M.C. with Capt. M°GRIGOR. R.A.M.C. following Brigade with instructions to join the Field Ambn attn known with each Bde and hup in touch with Regt M.O.'s + Brigade Headquarters — Head Qrs of Ambn remained at Armagh Camp MM# Instructions recvd fr. A.D.M.S. to Sea for Ambulance tn crown Division to run to Indian Hutin Hospital at AYETTE Proceeded to AYETTE and found all Indian + Indian Patients being transferred	

SECRET

WAR DIARY
or
INTELLIGENCE SUMMARY.
(Erase heading not required.)

Army Form C. 2118.

1/35 Field Ambulance
Vol XXII Page 6

Place	Date	Hour	Summary of Events and Information	Remarks and references to Appendices
			6th our buildings and premises to open as a Divisional Main Dressing Station filled up & used for receiving gassed cases with equipment brought away from Main Dressing Station ERVILLERS. Instructions received from A.D.M.S. to effect that O.C. 137 F.A. will be responsible for the evacuation of all casualties from Divisional front & Main Dressing Station AYETTE and will have Bearer Divisions of all three F.A.s at his disposal also all Ambulance Cars & Horsed Ambulance wagons — 30th M.O.C. will be responsible for evacuation of cases from M.D.S. to 43 C.C.S.	
AYETTE	23	6 p.m.	Opn. 26-D Cancelled. During night left night to 43 C.C.S. by M.O.C. cars – remaining wounded evacuated – all cars received A.T.S. and cleared down wounded —	
		12 m.n.	Number of cases since 8 a.m. becomes 47 wounded. D.D.M.S. VI Corps visits M.D.S.	
		8 A.M.	Return up to 8 a.m. 12 noon 162 including our gunners Cormier – steady flow of casualties sent in from COURCELLES also from Divisions on right. – Main Dressing Station GREVILLERS which is being closed – Enemy reported to have come through to ERVILLERS.	

Army Form C. 2118.

135 Field Ambulance
Vol XII Page 4

SECRET
WAR DIARY
or
INTELLIGENCE SUMMARY.
(Erase heading not required.)

Place	Date	Hour	Summary of Events and Information	Remarks and references to Appendices
AYETTE	1918 March 24th	12.30 a.m.	Message received from A.D.M.S. — to effect All horsed Transport to be in readiness to move at once — To be ready on receipt of report from O.C. 137 F.A. (O.C. being) to ebve as a M.D.S. and open as an Advanced Dressing Station — 136th F.A. to be prepared to act as a M.D.S. at MONCHIE au BOIS — Transport to be moved to MONCHY when Convenient expedient.	
AYETTE	25th		Capt. BEVERIDGE — Capt. McGREGOR approved went with bearer personnel via Boisleux Wallencourt to Fontaine — Transport out in to MONCHIE — AYETTE still run as main Dressing Station — nearly 400 casualties admitted during night — Runner obtained from D.D.M.S. VI Corps for evacuation of walking wounded to 43 C.C.S., Capt. Boroughs & bearers sent to report to O.C. 4th Div Bearers — 40 Divn M.A.C. Order No 56 dated 26.3.18 received — to effect 135th F.A. will hand over the M.D.S. & 1/2 East Lancs F.A. at once — on relief 135th F.A. will proceed to MONCHIE au BOIS — Infantry Bde will be relieved by 42nd Division tonight — O/C 137 F.A. will withdraw his Bearer Division & 40 Div in conjunction with Inf. Bde — on completion will march all to Div Bearers to MONCHIE au Bois when they will again form unit	

Army Form C. 2118.

SECRET

WAR DIARY or INTELLIGENCE SUMMARY

(Erase heading not required.)

135 Field Ambulance
Vol XXII Pages 8

Place	Date	Hour	Summary of Events and Information	Remarks and references to Appendices
	1916 March			
YETTE	25th	1 p.m.	Handed over D.M. Dummy Station & M 1/2 East Lancs F.A. together with all surplus equipment, platform blankets & 8 m stretchers — Practically all casualties now cleared at time of handing over — Dummy Lunnd 9 p.m. 22nd to 1 a.m. 25th. The following casualties passed through M.D.S. AYETTE Officers 40 Div 36 — Other Ranks 46 — Other Ranks 40 Div 755 — Other Ranks 965 — Total 1622 — MM4 Ambulance provided by march to MONCHY and formed up with Transport — Maj Brownely and majority of horses arrived at MONCHY — Ambulance proceeded to billets at RANSART — No. M.S. 554 Pte S.C. BREWER, A.S.C. M.T. was severely wounded, also driver in Ambulance car (whilst returning wounded) No.75069 Pte E. LANGFORD slightly wounded same time (manner of duty) Car was invented over by shell fire and could not be saved. — MM4	
RANSART				
POMMIER	26th		Ambulance marched out 9 a.m. to POMMIER — Two billets available — equipment Route settled for accommodation of personnel. Under instructions from A.D.M.S — One Officer Maj Brownely & 4 O.R. with horse Ambulance car reported at Hindsweller 12 m. Inf Bde with river	

SECRET

WAR DIARY
or
INTELLIGENCE SUMMARY.

Army Form C. 2118.

135 Field Ambulance
Vol XXII Page 9

Place	Date	Hour	Summary of Events and Information	Remarks and references to Appendices
	1918 March			
POMMIER			to helping sent parties with marquees to from Maj Burnley - to effect that he had arrived on O.D.S at S.H Comm of ADINFER WOOD mm 120th B.H Headquarters	
	26th		120th B.H Order No 183 16 3/15 received to effect Brigade will be withdrawn to Reserve on night of 26/27 & will move to HABARCQ - 135 Field Amb will move with Brigaded Units will form main column at 7 a.m at point near BEAUMETZ	
			RIVIERE Rd - cross ARRAS - DOULENS Rd	
WARLUZEL	27th		Ambulance arrived at 5 A.M on leaving BASSEUX - money received for Div Head Quarters. Their destination was changed to WARLUZEL - arrived WARLUZEL	
		11.30 a.m	In billets ourselves - equipment trucks followed for Pernand —	
	28th		Remained at WARLUZEL - 120th B.H Order No 184 28 3/15 received to effect	
			B.H Group will march to MONCHY BRETON area on 29th inst - 135 Field Ambulance will billet at LA THIEULOYE	
LA	29th		Marched with B.H to MONCHY BRETON and on to LA THIEULOY - to billets	
THIEULOYE	30th		120th B.H Warning Order received 2 a.m to effect 40 Divison is being transferred to XV Corps with a view to relieving 57th Division - 120 to B.H group	

SECRET

Army Form C. 2118.

WAR DIARY
or
INTELLIGENCE SUMMARY.
(Erase heading not required.)

135 Field Ambulance
Vol XXII Page 10

Place	Date	Hour	Summary of Events and Information	Remarks and references to Appendices
LA THIEULLOYE	1916 March 30th	9.45 am	will move by Army Order No 185 dated 30/3/18 Inf Bde Div No 185 dated 30/3/18 renew - 120th Bde Group will move by Sty to SAILLY SUR LYS - MONDE - own by Coy - entraining point in ST POL - BRUAY Road - at Road junction DIEVAL facing N.E. Detraining point ESTAIRES - NEUF BERQUIN road - 135 F.A. to march entraining point 10 a.m - First train Lienport to to Bruay and & move to LILLERS - much to be renewed on 31st to our own. Ambulance personnel marched to entraining point 10 a.m. & entrained & join Column at 12.30 p.m - Personnel arrived ESTAIRES - NEUF BERQUIN road and marched to SAILLY SUR LA LYS - Accommodation found for personnel by 2/2 East Lancs F.A. at Main Dressing Station.	
SAILLY SUR LA LYS	31st		40 Div Mvmt Order No 63 3/8 issued to effect 40 Div will relieve 57 Division on the line between 31st March & 2nd April x x & O.C. 135 F.A. will take over on April 1st from O.C. 2/2 Wessex F.A. the Main Dressing Station at DOULIEU (A.25.d.4.4.) and will reinv all sick from Divn — x x x Arrangements made with O.C. 2/2 Divn F.A. for relief and an advance	

SECRET

Army Form C. 2118.

WAR DIARY
or
INTELLIGENCE SUMMARY.
(Erase heading not required.)

135th Field Ambulance   Vol XXII   Part 11

Instructions regarding War Diaries and Intelligence Summaries are contained in F. S. Regs., Part II. and the Staff Manual respectively. Title pages will be prepared in manuscript.

Place	Date	Hour	Summary of Events and Information	Remarks and references to Appendices
BAILLY SUR LYS	1918 March 31st		Gratifying event to take over - Transport under Major BEVERIDGE arrived and marched straight to Main Dressing Station DOULIEU — AM	

B.M Kent Lieut Col R.A.M.C.
O.C 135th Field Ambulance

March 31st 1918

— Confidential —

War Diary

of

135th Field Ambulance

from April 1st 1918 to April 30th 1918.

— (volume XXIII). —

O.M.Hunt
Lieut Col R.A.M.C.
O.C. 135 Field Ambulance

WAR DIARY or INTELLIGENCE SUMMARY.

Army Form C. 2118.

135th Field Ambulance

VOL. XXIII Page 1

Place	Date	Hour	Summary of Events and Information	Remarks and references to Appendices
DOULIEU Map 36 A 25 d-4-4	1918 April 1st		Ambulance personnel marched from STRAZEELE via LYS to DOULIEU. Sit. When on from 2/3 Wessex Field Ambulance 59th Division - Relief completed at 12.30 p.m.	
"	2nd		Sick of Division all being admitted. Thin main dressing Station continued - Morning State - Running O.R. 17 - Admitted O.1. O.R. 52 = O.C.S. 2 - Duty 2.	
"			Linen Corp indentives - Thin O.B. M.S. 12 O.R. 841C forwarded to No. 54 C.C.S. for duty.	
"	3rd		Continued construction of work - Sickened. Morning State - Running - D.1. O.R. 35. Admitted O.R. 17. to C.C.S. 10 - Duty 1 - Weather very wet & damp.	
"	4th		Found return - Running. O.1 - O.R. 71 - admitted - O.2. O.R. 27 - to C.C.S. O.2 O.R. 12. to duty 3 - Allicher Conference at offices of A.D.M.S.	
"	5th		Weather still very wet - found in camp very muddy - Running. O.1. O.R. 83. Admitted O.R. 62 to C.C.S. O.1. O.R. 12. Duty 4	
"	6th		40 Division R.A.M.C. Order No 64 dated 5/4/15 received to effect Off 137 F.A. will hand over the A.D.S. & R.A.M.C. Posts in the Right Section to personnel of 136 F.A. on April 7th - O.C. 137 F.A. will continue to be responsible for evacuation of casualties from Divisional Front.	

WAR DIARY or INTELLIGENCE SUMMARY.

Army Form C. 2118.

135 2nd Field Ambulance
VOL XXIII Page 2

Place	Date	Hour	Summary of Events and Information	Remarks and references to Appendices
DOULIEU Sheet 36 A25 d.4-4	1916 April 6.		CAPT J. JARDINE. R.A.M.C. taken on strength of unit in addition to establishment on IV Corps A.D.M.S. — CAPT McGRIGOR R.A.M.C. posted for duty with 18th Welsh Regt & TRANS off strength — CAPT E.C. SPARROW — R.A.M.C. (T.C.) and CAPT. P. ALLEN R.A.M.C. (T.C.) arrived from 34th Division on 5/7/15 for duty — Morning State Running — OR.136. Admitted — O.3 - OR.48 — To CCS. 01 - OR.39 & Duty. Running O.2 — OR.134. — Instructions received that A.D.M.S. from D.D.M.S. Corps that 1Fld number of patients remaining in F.A. should not exceed 50 - arrangements made for clearing surplus cases — CAPT P. ALLEN posted to 136th F.A. for duty — MMB	
"	7"		Conferences at Cap. 3A.1 re establishment of Bearer Divisions of Ambulances. Morning State — Running 0-2 - OR.134 — Admitted 0-2 - OR 26 - To CCS 60 - OR.14 Running 0-2 - OR.79 — Weather fine - drying wind — MMB	
"	8"		Attended conference at A.D.M.S. Office re evacuation scheme, new area in case of retire-fighting — Morning State — Running - 0.2 - OR.79 - Admitted 21 - to CCS - 39 - & Duty 5 - Running 0-2 - OR.56 — Weather dull - showery — MMB	
"	9"		Heavy bombardment on front line started at 4.20 a.m —	
"		7.30 a.m.	Message received from O.D.M.S. asking if large Motor Ambulance to be sent to his office and one to	

WAR DIARY or INTELLIGENCE SUMMARY

Army Form C. 2118.

Unit: 135th Field Ambulance
Vol XVII page 3

Place	Date	Hour	Summary of Events and Information	Remarks and references to Appendices
GOMMIECOURT	1918 April			
	9th	8 a.m.	to R.A.P. Message from OC 137 F.A. asking if 135 F.A. would take Amb Cars to him - Cars wanted by R.A.P. - reported heavy bombardment with gas shells. We expect an infantry attack. MWE	
	9th	9.30 a.m.	Orders received from A.D.M.S. to send Bearer Division to report at once to Hintzgrafen 120th Inf Bdy to hand Amb wagons - an Officer to proceed at once to get in touch with H.Q. 2 - 120th B⁴ - 4 H wagons to act as Divisional Motor Dining Station and notify 2/c M₂ M A C when cars can return appointed to casualties wagons - MWE	
		10 a.m.	Maj Bromley proceeded to A.D⁴ 120th B⁴ and Bearer Division under Capt Allison complete followed MWE	
		11 a.m.	Report received from Maj Bromley (OC Bearers) to say he had got in touch with H.Qu 120 B⁴ and was sitting in touch with Battalions MWE	
		11.30	Report received from OC Bearers to say the head Quart ere an A.D.S. at 93.d.8.6 and relay by section M.B. Our loading point at 9.20.d.3.4. Lieut Farmerton 136 F.A. sent to A.D.S. - Wounded coming in - 5 M.O.s - N.C.O own for evacuation of wounded - Moving Cases the moment anything coming in - All wounded Walking Ambulance for 2 to 5 cases	

T2134. Wt. W708—776. 500000. 4/15. Sr. J.C. & S.

WAR DIARY or INTELLIGENCE SUMMARY

Army Form C. 2118.

135th Field Ambulance

VOL XXIII   Page 4

Place	Date	Hour	Summary of Events and Information	Remarks and references to Appendices
OULIEU			A.T.S. gear and Field Med Stores completed. Cars being evacuated to C.C.S. HAVERSKERQUE. Vans being loaded of walking wounded despatched to C.C.S.	
Strt 36				
A.25.d.4.4			136th Field Amb having abandoned Dressing Station at SAILLY 309 14. LYS came back to DOULIEU and opened a Walking Wounded Dressing Station near D.M.D.S. all walking wounded now double this.	
			Instructions received from A.D.S. that an hour in hand and Wagon was sent by skill Pin – but at 8 telephone from the wagon was sent back suffering from shell shock (NYDN) in attempting to get wagon across a burnt house we wounded and Serg. Diven A.S.C. wounded in arm (wagon had to be abandoned)	[signature]
		1.30 p.m.	O.C. Bearers reports all B.A.P. of 120th Bn. clear at 1.30 p.m.	
		2.30 p.m.	,, A.D.S. at Q.8.d.8.4 clear at 2.30 p.m.	
		6.30 p.m.	Steady flow of wounded coming on a evacuation taking place. 136 F.A. motor section from A.D.S. clear Walking Wounded Station at DOULIEU and proceed to VIEUX BERQUIN.	
,,		9 p.m.	Orders received from A.D.S. that D.M.D.S. at DOULIEU was to be closed as soon and cars to remain an A.D.S. – from there to be sent back to new D.M.D.S. opened	

Army Form C. 2118.

WAR DIARY
or
INTELLIGENCE SUMMARY.
(Erase heading not required.)

135th Field Ambulance

VOL XXIII Page 5

Instructions regarding War Diaries and Intelligence Summaries are contained in F.S. Regs., Part II. and the Staff Manual respectively. Title pages will be prepared in manuscript.

Place	Date	Hour	Summary of Events and Information	Remarks and references to Appendices
DOULIEU	1918 April		O/c 137 F.A at 9.44 Billet VIEUX BERQUOIN	
		1.4 p.m	Not many casualties coming through - further intensive shelling from V.D.N. & continue during evening. Clear about T.C.C.S to before on lorry or paddle AMB	
	10th	12.30 a.m	A fairly quiet night. Some again commenced coming in at 5 a.m. Enemy appeared to have broken through on the right and to be approaching DOULIEU — on information of same whilst it was decided to withdraw ambulance together from DOULIEU — Col D.D.M.S sent present to VIEUX BERQUOIN — Transport detachment sent on with only medical equipment etc in panier and laden by ambulance. O.C Command Brown sent Col Ambulance Brown main left W. Col DOULIEU with sufficient personnel to continue on A.D.S. until enemy in essentials to VIEUX BERQUOIN — Personnel withdrawn from camp at 12 noon - Proceeded on but car to repart to A.D.M.S at VIEUX BERQUOIN and arranged location for Ambulance RMZ	
VIEUX BERQUOIN		2 p.m	Ambulance arrived at VIEUX BERQUOIN and finished near Crossroad of 136 F.A	
		2.30 p.m	136 F.A. proceeded to STRAZEELE and opened up a D.M.S in School	

WAR DIARY or INTELLIGENCE SUMMARY

Army Form C. 2118.

135th Field Ambulance
Vol. XXIII
Page 6.

Place	Date	Hour	Summary of Events and Information	Remarks and references to Appendices
	1916 April			
			O.C. had been in c/m of scheme covering to reinforce D.M.D.S. at VIEUX BERQUIN 9am	
	10th	4 pm	Orders received from A.D.M.S. Ambulance to proceed to STRAZEELE and there reinf 136 F.A.	
		5 pm	left VIEUX BERQUIN for STRAZEELE —	
STRAZEELE		6.9 pm	arrived STRAZEELE — started transport via 136 F.A. Tincques and obtained billets for Ambce. Comm and ment in farms near villge	
HAZEBROUCK (SHEET 4)			Note: Total number of casualties which passed thro D.M.D.S. DOULIEU from 10 a.m. to 9 pm 6.12 noon to 10th inst = 640 — ie 40 Divn Officers 23 - other Ranks 8 — Other ranks 40th Divn 361 other Divns 224 — Refugees from 17 — French civilians 4 — MWB Ambulances on billets STRAZEELE — One M.O. detached by motor ambulance and one NCO order car by hand ambulance rigger to reinforce Senior Officer in DOULIEU — hand ambulance for A.D.M.S. casualties road between STRAZEELE	
	11th		HAZEBROUCK to first available bid for opening a D.M.D.S if required 136 F.A. handed over D.M.D.S. as STRAZEELE to an Ambulance of 31st Divn and proceeded to join its Bde — 137 moved from VIEUX BERQUIN to PRADELLES — Instructions received from A.D.M.S. for 135 F.A. to remain in billets	

WAR DIARY
INTELLIGENCE SUMMARY

Army Form C. 2118.

135th Field Ambulance
VOL XXIII   Page 7

Place	Date	Hour	Summary of Events and Information	Remarks and references to Appendices
STRAZEELE	1916 April 11th		Quin STRAZEELE for the present	
HAZEBROUCK SHEET (4)		10 a.m	Warning Order (A.D.M.S. verbal) for unit to march with 12th Yorkshire Regt. (Pioneers) this morning (as soon as orders are received) for Division to withdraw from the line.) Orders to march to HAZEBROUCK — Further orders — F.A. will move on Wednesday morning of 12th April — marching at 6 a.m. — rendezvous ½ a mile north of HAZEBROUCK. Off main road — x x Entrainment of troops unable to walk will commence 12 noon accommodation for F.A. being allotted on 2nd train x x Old Transport & Limbered proceeding by march route not known in order of march L.of C road WALLON-CAPPEL & EBBLINGHEM — on night of 12/13 continue march on 13th to destination ARQUES area —	
	12th		Ambulance paraded at 6 a.m. in order for HAZEBROUCK — received intimation from Staff Officer 40th Div. that move was cancelled — limits to remain as before — returned to billets STRAZEELE — instructions received from A.D.M.S. awaiting move of	
		12 noon	F.A. — O.C. Personnel and remainder of teams upon their return - being transport awaits orders to WALLON before further move from STRAZEELE	
		1.30 pm	Instructions received from A.D.M.S. to effect F.A. will move at once and park on side of road & La Hte Loge — LES CISEAUX Road (N.W. of HAZEBROUCK) in order	

Army Form C. 2118.

135th Field Ambulance
VOL XXIII   Page 8

WAR DIARY or INTELLIGENCE SUMMARY.
(Erase heading not required.)

Place	Date	Hour	Summary of Events and Information	Remarks and references to Appendices
STRAZEELE	1918 April 12th		from N to S - 135 - 136 - 137 - F.A. will be prepared to move as soon as the shortest notice xx on the work of the Division entraining engineer OC 137 F.A. will be responsible for the evacuation of casualties AMB	
HONDEGHEM (HAZEBROUCK SHEET) (3)		3 a.m.	Ambulance left STRAZEELE - Detachment of Ambulance arrived at HONDEGHEM by motor ambulance arrived from DADS on route - Instructions for transport and billets for personnel found on farm on HONDEGHEM - STAPLES (just over 1st C in LES CISEAUX) — 136 F.A. opened a D.M.D.S. on school Baan office sent to report to OC 137 F.A. — 136 F.A. opened a D.M.D.S. on school from HONDEGHAM — AMB	
"	13th		On billets HONDEGHAM - All motor ambulances sent to OC 137 F.A. for his disposal in sharing evacuation for 40 Div line of regiment	
		2 p.m.	Message from ADMS received. All units will be prepared to move on their transport lines o.c.o - Detachment sent - horses will follow - F.A. personnel with evacuation at HONDEGHAM when infantry moves from present position — AMB	
"		8 p.m.	Verbal instructions received from 9.S.O.2. 40 Div - Ambulances to march Enigma with 120 B.M. to ZUYPTEEN billets & recommence march in morning to area west of ST OMER - Ambulance wounded staff of F.Am. sent into billets	

135th Field Ambulance
VOL XXIII Page 9

Place	Date 1915 April	Hour	Summary of Events and Information	Remarks and references to Appendices
ZUYPTEEN	14.		Found by billeting officer over ZUYPTEEN at 2 am AW	
HAZEBROUCK (SHEET) (F) ②		6 am	Orders received from A.D.M.S. & B.O. 120 Brigade to march to ST OMER -	
		10 am	Marched at rear of 120 Bth to ST OMER - rested at 1 pm no billets available - Bth O.C. W. to ST OMER - accommodation found in P of W Camp for which permission was eventually given soon - (CAPT SORROW R.A.M.C. conducted to No.X Station.) AW	
ST OMER (D) ③	15"		Ambulance located in P of W Camp. AW	
	16"		At rest from 120 Bth (estimated around ETTINGUEM) AW Instructions received from 40 Div at 12.2 - that an area billeting accommodation being allotted to 120 Bth - 135 F.A. will move to Brigade Area - Transport repacked in readiness AW	
		9 am	Had a disc. just received from H.Qr 120 Bth & to new location & ambulance	
		7 pm	Verbal instructions received from Staff Capt 120 B.9. that billets accommodation was allotted at LONGUENESSE - Billeting Officers dispatched to investigate	
LONGUENESSE ④	17 th		Ambulance moved at 10 a.m. to billets in LONGUENESSE - Equipment unpacked for instructing injuries & vehicles etc. M.O. horses & Detachm. Ward (Army)	

WAR DIARY or INTELLIGENCE SUMMARY.

Army Form C. 2118.

135th Field Ambulance   Page 10
VOL XXIII

Place	Date	Hour	Summary of Events and Information	Remarks and references to Appendices
LONGUENESSE	1918 April 17		in school room – All available Officers attended to D.M.S. conference at 137 F.A. AMB	
	18		Wagon painting etc continued AMB	
		2.30 A.M	G.O.C. 40th Division inspected personnel of F.A. & addressed them informing him adjustments of the rank & file in recent operations – AMB	
	19"		In billets LONGUENESSE – AMB	
	20		Warning Order received from ADMS 40 Div that 40 Div be in Head Quarters – Div RA Composite Brigade & 40 Div MT Coy will move to BOISDINGHEM area tomorrow F.A. & E min under orders from Three Brigades – AMB	
			120th by Bth Order No 192 21/5 received Sixty details of more – 135 F.A. & more to LA POUVRE – Billeting Officers sent on to meet Staff Captain at BOISDINGHEM – AMB	
	21st	2 P.M	Left LONGUENESSE marched with 121 B.G. & ACQUIN	
E. POUVRE (ACQUIN)		5.30 P.M	Arrived in billets LE POUVRE – AMB	
	22"		In billets – Transport improved to continue refitting permitting etc – AMB	
AZEBROUCK SHEET B 4	25"		Arrangements made for collection and disposal of over 9 120 B" AMB	
	26"		Still at LE POUVRE – Issued uniform AMB	
			do do AMB	

WAR DIARY
INTELLIGENCE SUMMARY

135th Field Ambulance

VOL XXIII Page 11

Army Form C. 2118.

Place	Date	Hour	Summary of Events and Information	Remarks and references to Appendices
E. POORE (ACQUIN)	1915 April 27th	2.30 a.m.	40 Divnm RAMC order No. 65 26/4/15 received. In effect — orders received from Second Army that Divl Headquarters & two Composite Bdes formed from 40th Div are placed at disposal of VIII Corps — No 1 Composite to consist of all troops not formed with 121st Corps Bde (including 137 F.A.) — No 2 Comp. Bde to consist of A/22, 119 Bde, "A" Bde, 18th Bdes RFA "B" Bde, 13 Sub Survey Regt — "C" Bde, H/32, + 2 Coys 14 HFE1 + 2 Coys 14 HF 2nd No 2 Coy Div Train — 1 Coy 40th Bn Bde Q.C. and 136th Field Ambulance — OC 135 F.A. will detail 3 Medical officers + 2 horse Ambulance cars & what to OC 136 F.A. by 9 a.m. April 27th	
"	"	8.30 a.m.	Maj W.R.P. McNEIGHT — Capt. B.P. HANSON and Lieut MEALON, U.S.M.C. & two horse Ambulance cars reported to 136 F.A.	
"	28th		Ambulance still awaiting orders in billets LE POORE	
"	29th	9.30 p.m.	40 Divnm RAMC Order No 66 received. In effect. No 2 Composite Brigade will move to Camp vacated by No 1 Composite Bde × R.W.E.L.D. ×× Troops not included in Composite Bde + Div H2" (vide RACD Order No 65) will move to LUMBRES. Ammn Column, also will be moved later × 135 F.A. will detach two horse Ambulances & report to O.C. 136 F.A. by 6 a.m. 30th inst.	

Army Form C. 2118.

WAR DIARY
or
INTELLIGENCE SUMMARY.
(Erase heading not required.)

135th Field Ambulance
VOL XXIII Page 12

Instructions regarding War Diaries and Intelligence Summaries are contained in F. S. Regs., Part II. and the Staff Manual respectively. Title pages will be prepared in manuscript.

Place	Date	Hour	Summary of Events and Information	Remarks and references to Appendices
LA POUVRE	1916 April 30	12 noon	120th Bde Order No 194 received – Bde group will move to LUMBRES area	
			Relay – Brigade H.Qrs & LUMBRES remainder to SENNINGHEM – two to move independently	
		2.30 pm	Ambulance left LE POUVRE & march to SENNINGHEM	
SENNINGHEM		4 pm	Took over billets – 6.30 p.m. J.W. McINTOSH RAMC (T.F.) posted to unit for duty	

30-4-16

J.M. Munro Lieut Col RAMC
OC 135 Field Ambulance

135TH FIELD AMBULANCE.

Confidential.

War Diary

of

135 Field Ambulance

from May 1/18 to May 31/18

(volume XXIV)

Lieut Col RAMC
O.C. 135 Field Ambulance

Army Form C. 2118.

135th Field Ambulance
VOL - XXIV   Page - 1 -

WAR DIARY
or
INTELLIGENCE SUMMARY.
(Erase heading not required.)

Place	Date	Hour	Summary of Events and Information	Remarks and references to Appendices
SENINGHAM	1918 May 1st		In billets. Brought into details of 120th B.A.	
HAZEBROUCK SHEET	2nd	1 a.m.	Details of personnel to be retained as running cadre in the rest of the Ambulance ordered to train as Advanced Dressing Unit - received from A.D.M.S.	
(A)		6 a.m.	Wire received from 120th B.A. to notify that all units of 120th B.A. Group will move to WATTEN (N. of St OMER) tomorrow (details to be issued later) Orders of standard carried out.	
"		12 midnight	Wire from 120th B.A. & Office that an instructions from Division move is postponed to 4th inst.	
"	3rd		Unit remained at SENINGHAM - Instructions received from A.D.M.S. - 8 Officers that no accommodation being available into 120th B.A. at WATTEN - unit was to join 137th F.A. in ST MOMELIN area - 40 in Div R.T.C. order no 67 3/5 received (calling for similar when in detail on 8th inst)	
"	4th		Orders instructions from A.D.M.S. May. J.W. MCINTOSH MADC (T.F.) on duty that 136th F.A. to be put on to report to A.D.M.S. 29th Divn.	
INDER BELCH HAZEBROUCK SHEET		8.30 a.m.	Ambulance formed by smaller roads to ST MOMELIN area - arrived 3.45 p.m. - Personnel arranged etc - in equipment took - in bivvy near KINDERBECK -	
3.D.6.3			Capt ALLINSON doing temp duty with 136 F.A. was posted from that unit to 29th Div.	

WAR DIARY
INTELLIGENCE SUMMARY

Army Form C. 2118.

135th Field Ambulance
Vol. XXIV   Page - 2 -

Place	Date	Hour	Summary of Events and Information	Remarks and references to Appendices
INDERBIELCH HAZEBROUCK SHEET 3.D.6.8.	1916 May 5		Units carried on W.R.P.T. Night lignal galway after comp duty with 136 F.A. Completion of duty with 137 F.A. - Ambulances attended Ceremonial Parade with 120th B.de at WATTEN for presentation of medal ribbon for conspicuous gallantry in connection with operations 21st & 25th March - Sergt DARDENNE G.S.C. M.T. & Corpl BUSBOROUGH R.A.M.C. bar awarded Military Medals - MMB	
	6		Capt HUSPROTT R.A.M.C. joined ambulance & took instructions for A.D.M.S from Gen'l on E 136 F.A. & to connect to A.D.M.S. & 29th Division - Lieut M'ALDON being temp attd with 136 F.A. was also posted to 29th Div - MMB	
			Very heavy rain during night - Camp very wet - CAPT M'CARTER MC RAMC joined ambulance for 14th F.A.1 & was transferred to A.D.M.S. 9th Div. - Corpl M'LARIN L'LIEUT. LA ROTUNDA 11'S	
	7th		D.C. joined out over transport to 6th Division — MMB	
			Administration Information concerning the WINNIZEELE LINE received from 42d & 40 Division	
	8		40th Division DAMC Warning Order No. 6.2 date 8.5.16 received to effect F.A. of 40th Divn will be responsible for sewing first Sanitary Change of troops arriving in Corps Sector, in connection with M.O.s of 31st & 35th Labour Groups - Do commanding F.A. will submit to this Comn every Friday 1 Staff Sergt & Clerk and 6 men for duty at the Dummy Station of this instructor - relabel	

WAR DIARY or INTELLIGENCE SUMMARY

Army Form C. 2118.

135th Field Ambulance
Vol. XXIV Page 3

Place	Date	Hour	Summary of Events and Information	Remarks and references to Appendices
KINDERBELCH	May 1918 8"		1 Hey Amb Car & Ford Car & 1 Motor Wagon will be allotted for duty with this Amb	
HAZEBROUCK SHEET			who will be accommodated in 1 Operating tent & 1 Bell tent pitched by this inspection	
			Ambulance – Orders to be held in readiness to move at short notice – 13.6.F.A. will be	
3.D.6.8			responsible for A & B Sections – 137 C Section & 135 D Section –	
			Instructions issued for A.D.M.S. to meet M.O. of 75th Salvas Group at Cross Roads	
			WINNIZEELE on timing of visit at 2 p.m. to quote preliminary measurements regarding	
			disposal of the sick etc – a position for Collecting Station to be chosen with the view	
		9 "	of connecting & clearing cases to ARNEKE –	
	9"		Arrangements made with the O.C. 75th Salvas Group. All Walking Compenses to proceed on	
			"D" Section in Charras. Site for Collecting During Diversion selected at KEINEN PIT	
		11.30 am	C 30 b 4.7 — & 40 1m RAMC Ditto at 69 dor 9.5 secured also Medicine Dressings of Station	
	10 "		Maj D. Wright with detachment proceeded to C.30.6.4.7. & allotters Dressing Station	
			Arrangements & F.A. Division at KINDERBELGH –	
	11 "		Small detachment at KEIKEN PIT	
	12 "		Unit Still in the Environs of KINDERBELGH –	
	13 "		Much the reconnaissance & work the M. of Division – WINNEZEELE are	

WAR DIARY
or
INTELLIGENCE SUMMARY.

Army Form C. 2118.

135th Field Ambulance
Vol XXIV Page 4

Place	Date	Hour	Summary of Events and Information	Remarks and references to Appendices
	1918 May			
HINDENBERG	15th		with view of preparation of Indirect Defence Scheme - weather much drier	
GAZE BRANCH SHEET	16th		Moved Armament from Ends to Ellis in a forward zone	
3.D.C.8			Ambulance still resting - Brothers Religion still Frequent burials - airmount at MM	
	19th		do do Warm dry weather	
	22nd		Hymnal weather - Preparation of Defence schemes continued	MM
	23rd		Renewed employed under R.E. digging - Fine weather continues	MM
	24th		Warm weather - a hot day	MM
	26th		No change - weather again hot	MM
	"	12.30 pm	Instructions received from Head Quarters 40th Div to effect that the Training Cadres	
			of 135th & 136th Field Ambulance will move by road on 28th May to join 4th American Infantry Division at SAMER - Training Cadre consists of Officer Commanding Officer, Quartermaster, Sergt Major, 2 Staff Sergts, 3 Sergeants (Benn) 1 Sergt Clerk, 15 other ranks (for preliminary training of American personnel as- This personnel will be shown eg. strength from date of departure	MM
	27th		40th Division D.M.C orders No. 10 April 27th issued - Also Training Cadre rolls complete. Home and Hebei transfer full O.S.C. 1147 - R.P. and M.T. & R.E. personnel	

WAR DIARY or INTELLIGENCE SUMMARY

Army Form C. 2118.

of 135th Field Ambulance Vol. XXIV Page 5

Place	Date	Hour	Summary of Events and Information	Remarks and references to Appendices
	1918 May			
INDER BOSCH			was fired on by machine gun at 9 a.m. on 28th May & respect to Headquarters Field Ambulance Divisn at SAMER on 29th May. Both F.A. to march under orders	
AZEBROUCK SHEET 3 D 6.6			of C 135 F.A. who will respect departure to this office — x x Surplus personnel of 135 and /36 F.A. will come under the Comy of 137 F.A. and will be accommodated in Tents at Krankestellen — O.C. 1/2 Dressing Station of 135 and 136 F.A. will carry on at present under orders of O.C. 137 F.A. —	
			40th Divn Headquarters No 818(R) award his (C.B.M.'s x x Haig's announcer Nyne 26/27th May BAYENGHEM-LES-SENINGHEM (Appreciation) x x who F Dave Commanded LUMBRES on day in advance — Regd 29/30th Divy SAMER. Appreciation to respect to 4th Canadian Divy A.D.M.S and also Comn Drove and Divn in advance — Officer commanding 1/2 F.A. will respect around to 4th Canadian Divn SAMER — Return for concentration from 30th May will be issued — x x x MME	
	29	6 p.m	Instructions received from A.D.M.S. that on concentration 135 & 136 F.A. will respect L.A.D.M.S. 16 th Division on arrival at SAMER inctead of 4th Canadian Divsn. Two laz Field Ambulance Cars against went on completion of Company duty with 52nd Division —	

WAR DIARY or INTELLIGENCE SUMMARY

Army Form C. 2118.

135th Field Ambulance

Vol XXIV Page 6

Place	Date	Hour	Summary of Events and Information	Remarks and references to Appendices
SAMETTE (LUMBRES)	1918 May 28th		Training Cadre of unit with Motorlorries transport full line Motor transport arrived at 9 a.m. from KINDERBELIE and arrived at letter allotted by Corps Commander LUMBRES – at SAMETTE (LUMBRES) at 4 p.m. – MM	
	29th		135, 136 F.A. report SAMETTE at 8 a.m. with orders to hold men DESVRES for medical insp. and evac. when O.C. who proceeded to report to A.D.M.S. 16 Dn. a SANER & EXCELLENT demonstrat.: make billeting arrangements - Billeting arrangements completed for 135 F.A. at EMAUIN, 135 F.A. at WIRWIGNES – Ambulance arrived Samette at 3 p.m. arrived WIRWIGNES – from – Information received from A.D.M.S. that	
WIRWIGNES CALAIS SHEET 4.D.2.4	30th		Army Co Common Medical Unit for Training. and heavy job awaits. Supplies provided of 7 F.As will rejoin – Correspond & to units to rest & refitting transport for Unit on 30th inst. a 6 p.m. at OUTREAU Sections (near BOULOGNE) MM	
	31st		In billets and under Corps at WIRWIGNES Maj D.S. BEVERIDGE & 136 other ranks Ambulance personnel reported unit at 12 midnight	

(D) M Monk Lieut Col Name
O 135th Field Ambulance

W 25
140/307c

135TH
FIELD
AMBULANCE.
No.
Date

Confidential

War Diary

of

135 Field Ambulance

from June 1/18 to June 30/18.

(volume 25)

June 30th
1918

O M Hunt Lieut Col RAMC
O.C. 135 Field Ambce

Army Form C. 2118.

135th Field Ambulance
Vol XXV Page - 1 -

WAR DIARY
or
INTELLIGENCE SUMMARY.
(Erase heading not required.)

Place	Date	Hour	Summary of Events and Information	Remarks and references to Appendices
WIRWIGNES	1918 June 1st		Ambulance (with 16th Division) in Camp & billets at WIRWIGNES - MMW	
	2nd		Maj W.R.P. McNEIGHT returned from temporary duty with 137th & A 40th Division	
CALAIS (SHEET)	3rd		A Dump Station in Carvoin opened for reception of sick from 56th American Inf. Regt. now	
4 D.2.4			attached with us recently - in accordance with the A.D.M.S. 16th Division to S.192/257 2/6/18. Instead	
			Arrangements - A large number of personnel of Ambulance working sick into Epidemic	
			Influenza - MMW	
	4/5		Trend continues - numbers & cases of influenza increasing - extra tent tents opened for -	
	6/5		Sick cases still being felt attend - Two cases of mumps (American troops) remain - influenza	
			epidemic in unit continues - MMW	
	8/6		Trend continues - numbers & cases of influenza etc - under instruction from A.D.M.S - 2 hund	
			Ambulance wagons reported to 1st Bn 2nd B. 56th American Inf Regt - to proceed with rest on	
			the march on the 9th inst - Union Water Cart Ambulance reported to 16th Div M.T. Coy for temporary	
	9th		duty with units with train - MMW	
	"		56th American Infantry Regt. left our lines - units of 320th Am Inf Regt. took our billets	
			Arrangements made for clearing sick - 319th Am Inf Regt arrived in DESVRES area	
			Arrangements made with M.O., Regt 142nd for collection & sick	

WAR DIARY or INTELLIGENCE SUMMARY

Army Form C. 2118.

135th Field Ambulance
VOL XXV Page 2

Place	Date	Hour	Summary of Events and Information	Remarks and references to Appendices
	1918 June			
WIRWIGNES	10th		Four G.S. Wagons detailed for duty with 16th Div. Train for employing duty in Ambulance with unhorsed. Guard from H.Q.D.M.S. MWB	
CALAIS SHEET 4 D 2.6	11th		Handed over Command of Ambulance to Major A.J. BEVERIDGE RC name on Ambulance for employing duty as acting A.D.M.S. 16th Division. AMHunt Lieut Col RAMC	
	13th		Routine work. mostly of interest to report. AJB	
	15th		Routine work, Influenza epidemic prevalent. Stopped only fine of 16 unit in hospital to day - down services patients. AJB	
	17th		Lieut Col A.M.HUNT RAMC rejoined on completion of temp duty as A.D.M.S. 16th Div and resumed command of unit. This came under command of G.O.C. 34th Division at 7 p.m. - Headquarters of 16th Division having departed from area in route for England.	
	19th		Warning orders received from A.D.M.S. 34th Division "Be prepared to move at short notice to another area" Preparations made for storing clean Divisional Station MWB	
	20th		2nd Warning order received from A.D.M.S. 34th Division - Unit will be prepared to move	

Army Form C. 2118.

WAR DIARY or INTELLIGENCE SUMMARY.
(Erase heading not required.)

135th Field Ambulance
Vol XXV Page 3

Place	Date	Hour	Summary of Events and Information	Remarks and references to Appendices
WIRWIGNES	1918 June 22nd		In a rest area on June 22nd. MWB	
CALAIS SHEET 44 D 2.4	23rd		34th Division RAMC Order No 63 23/6 received - to effect 135th and 136th Field Ambulance will rejoin the 40th Division on under June 24th. 135 FA from WIRWIGNES to QUERCAMP - & report on arrival to Asst Commandant BOIS DINGHAM - x x MWB	
	24th		June 25th. 135 FA from QUERCAMP to HQrs 119th Inf Bde. Unit proceeded by march route with lorries WIRWIGNES at 9 am. arrived in billets QUERCAMP	
QUERCAMP		5.30 pm	Orders received from ADMS 40th Division - you will move on 25th inst to a site selected on RENESCURE-EBBLINGHAM Road - Sheet 27/T 22.a.3.4 x x MWB	
	25th		Left QUERCAMP by march route at 9 am. arrived at RENESCURE (T 22.a.3.4) 4.30 pm. Personnel billetted in town barn - Site area Divn Hospital Marquees pitched (out of Walking Wounded Collecting Station - XV Corps - Ambulances received from DMS XV Corps time ADMS to effect 10 Sub.Com P.M. marquees with annex for 135 FA & holds these marquees and proved to form a WWCS ambulance for HTD cases - MWB	
22.a.3.4 Sheet 24	26th		33 ORs admit camp Contradiction of camp proceeded with - Lorries used on a Divny Station for such of them Bns of 40th Divn - 137 FA will move to site of Corps Walking Wounded Collecting	
	27th		Orders received from ADMS 40 Div -	

WAR DIARY or INTELLIGENCE SUMMARY

Army Form C. 2118.

135th Field Ambulance
Vol XVIV Page 4

Place	Date	Hour	Summary of Events and Information	Remarks and references to Appendices
"	1918 June			
	27th		Station at 27/T 22 a 3.4 on 25th inst. 135 F.A. will move to selected site at 36 A/B 18 C.0.0 on same day. The whole Field amb to meet & entrain as M.D.S. 40th Division R.A.M.C. order No 16 dated 27-6-18 received. – 6 officers "RAMC Order No 74 + Ambulances are cancelled." In event of an enemy attack on 2nd Army front the 40th Division and attached troops will man the West Hazebrouck line from 36/D 25 c & 29/V 6 central × × × "Div Head Qrs in rest RENESCURE 27/T 21 a 1.0." × × × Southern section – 120th Bde. B.H.Q. at 36A/C 21 d 0.3 – S Boundary a line drawn from D 26 c 4.3 – D 25 d 3.5 – C 29 d 5.8 to C 26 c 4.3 – N Boundary C.6 – d 8.2 – C.6 a 0.6 – C.5 d 0.3 – C.4 d 6.2 – C.3 d 2.0. C.2 d 0.7 – O.C. 135th Field Ambulance will be responsible for the evacuation of all casualties from Southern Sector – A.D.S. will be established at 36A/C 14. a 1.0 × × × 135 F.A. will entrain & MDS for Southern Corner at 36 A/B 18. C.0.0 × × ×	MM
6. A/ B.16 C.0.0	28th		Handed over site & lighter equipment etc of D.W.C.S. at T 22 a 34 at 13.75 F.A. proceeded to field at farm 36.A/B.18. C.0.0. & pitching camp – Tour Marquees & one bell tents in addition to Ambulance equipment lent – Interviewed Area Commandant & re No 49 Sanitary Sect re Sanitary Arrangements. etc	MM

T2134. Wt. W708—776. 500000. 4/15. Sir J. C. & S.

Army Form C. 2118.

WAR DIARY
or
INTELLIGENCE SUMMARY.

135th Field Ambulance

Vol. XV Page 5

(Erase heading not required.)

Place	Date	Hour	Summary of Events and Information	Remarks and references to Appendices
36 A	1918 June 30th		Ambulance work & preparations of Main Dressing Station as normal — Inchant Imperant	
B 16 C.O.O.			ADS & RAP for front of line to be recommended by this event — EMMA	
WARINGHEM				

A M Hunt Lieut Col
R.A.M.C.
O/C 135 Field Ambulance

135TH FIELD AMBULANCE.

Confidential

War Diary

of

135th Field Ambulance.

from July 1/18 to July 31/18.

(volume XXVI).

Lieut Col Rame
O.C. 135 Fd. Ambulance

WAR DIARY

135th Field Ambulance
Volume 26 - Page - 1

Army Form C. 2118

Place	Date	Hour	Summary of Events and Information	Remarks and references to Appendices
36 A	1916 July 1st		In Camp. Routine work - No patients being admitted to Main Dressing Station, all sick sent back to 120th B'de Clearing & conveyed to M D S of 136 F A	Init.
B.19.C.o.o			The following names of personnel of this unit - published in Kings Birthday Honours together with Routine order of 40th Division with "Military Medal" Majr L Crawford MC (now of 136 FA) "Mention"- Majr W R P McKnight "Mention" - No 59373 Sergt W Muller "Meritorious Service Medal"	
BLARINGHEM	2nd		No 71496 Pte E F Wood - Meritorious Service Medal. Joined unit - Capt T R Trounce RAMC reported on discharge from No 36 C C S Nothing of importance to record - Weather continues dry + warm -	Init. Init.
"	4th 6th		Lieut O A G Brooks - H L Hill and L F Miller - M O R C U S A posted to unit for duty. One hundred children twice from 64th Labour Group- inspected as to physical fitness and enlisted in British Army -	Init.
"	9th 10th 11th		Under instructions from D.D.M.S XV Corps Lieuts H L Hill + R M Miller - M O R C proceeded to report EADMS 29th Division for duty and are struck off strength of unit	Init.
	12th		Lieut Quartermaster T Wood RAMC arrived from 2/3 N Midland Fd Ambulance and is taken on the strength of this unit -	Init.
	14th		Capt T R Trounce RAMC detached for temporary duty as M.O to 15 KOYLI	Init.

WAR DIARY
or
INTELLIGENCE SUMMARY
(Erase heading not required.)

Army Form C. 2118.

135th Field Ambulance

Vol = 26 - Page 2

Place	Date	Hour	Summary of Events and Information	Remarks and references to Appendices
	1916 July			
36A	16th		Cloud nimbus. weather dull dry & warm. G.O.C. 40th Div inspected Ambulance	
B.18.C.O.0	19th		and orders of Margum Harman from O.D.M.S. and instructions made for receiving and treating Scabies & impetigo cases for Division – 4 cases Scabies transferred from 137 F.A.	
BLARINGHEM	20th		All linings being dug out 2 bivouacs made for protection against splinters from bombs from enemy aircraft —	
	22nd		Cloud nimbus – some rain —	
	24th	at RACQUINHEM	Arrangements made for collecting sick from 2nd Australian Brigade – change from E 136th F.A. for strength & 1st Australian D.R.S.	
	26th		Lieut J L PHIBBS R.A.M.C. (T.C.) arrived for duty and is taken on the strength	
			20 reinforcements O.R. arrived from Calais Base Depot and are taken on strength	
	27th		Capt E H RAINEY R.A.M.C. posted for duty is taken on strength –	
	29th		Cloud nimbus — Very heavy rain	
	30th		Such instructions from D.M.S. Arrangements made with O.C. 2/3 Scott Midland Field Ambulance 61st Division for taking over F.A. at 36A/B.28 0-2.5	

Army Form C. 2118.

WAR DIARY
~~INTELLIGENCE~~ SUMMARY

135th Field Ambulance
Vol 26 Page 3

(Erase heading not required.)

Instructions regarding War Diaries and Intelligence Summaries are contained in F. S. Regs., Part II. and the Staff Manual respectively. Title pages will be prepared in manuscript.

Place	Date	Hour	Summary of Events and Information	Remarks and references to Appendices
	1918			
36 A	July		Major W.R.P. McNeight, Capt. T.R. Trounce proceeded with our tent subdivision	
B18.c.6.0	31st		to later on the orders of the Corps Main Depot at 36 A 28 - a 2.5	
BLA RINGHEN				

J.M. Hawk Lieut Col RAMC
OC 135 F.A.

Vol 27
140/3200

135TH FIELD AMBULANCE.
No........
Date........

COMMITTEE FOR THE
MEDICAL HISTORY OF THE WAR
Date 5 OCT 1918

Confidential War Diary

of

135 Field Ambulance

from Aug 1/18 to Aug 31/18

(volume XXVII)

Aug 1/18
16

B.M.Hunt
Lieut Col & Cmd
O.C. 135 Fd. Ambulance

Army Form C. 2118.

WAR DIARY
or
INTELLIGENCE SUMMARY

(Erase heading not required.)

135 Field Ambulance
Vol 27. Page 1.

Place	Date	Hour	Summary of Events and Information	Remarks and references to Appendices
	1918 Aug			
36 A	1st		Usual routine at Headquarters Detachment at XV Corps Skin Centre carrying on	
B 19	2nd		construction work —	
C.O.O.	3rd		For reinforcements two rank & file and rent from Cyclist Base Depot	
CLARINGHEM	4th		Lieut J L PHIBBS R.A.M.C. attached for temporary duty on M.S.S. 13th East Lanc. Regt	
	6th		Lieut L.T.H. CALDWELL R.A.M.C. posted to unit from 10th K.O.S.B.s and taken on strength — Establishment of Officers now complete	
	8th		All Orns of Section remaining Wimereux & XV Corps Skin Centre —	
	9th		Two G.D. Orderlies attached for temp duty at CHATEAU LANNOY LUMBRES	
			One nursing orderly to XV Corps Legn(?) School and one nursing orderly & 2 O.Rs	
			XV Corps —	
	10th		Band writin — weather continue hot & dry	
	12th		Lieut A.G. BROOKS R.O.R.C. detached for temporary duty with 11th Bn	
			Cameron Highlanders — Lieut J L PHIBBS R.A.M.C. from temp duty	
			with 13th East Lancs to 23rd Bn Cheshire Regt for temporary duty —	
	13th		Two O.R. returned from temporary duty at Ambulance Training LUMBRES	

WAR DIARY
or
INTELLIGENCE SUMMARY.

135th Field Ambulance
Vol 27 Page 2

Army Form C. 2118.

Place	Date	Hour	Summary of Events and Information	Remarks and references to Appendices
	June			
36A	14		Major A J BEVERIDGE M.C. RAMC proceeded to UK on 14 days leave. MMM	
B.16	15		No 1/2 SR/02865 S/Sergt Major C B HARRINGTON - QSC HT rejoined unit from hospital	
C.0.0	16		No 39837 Q M S B LAMBERT granted rank of Warrant Officer Class II Army Order No 194 1916 from 22nd June 1918. MMM	
HARINGHEM	21st		Order instructions from ADMS concerning ADS and forward posts of 94th Field Amb.	
"			31st Division -	
			40th Division D.A.M.C. Order No 83 dated 21/6/18 received to effect "40 Division will take over front now held by 31st Division - The front to be taken over will be from the XV Corps Southern Boundary to the Plat Buque River at F.14.a.3.5 (Sheet 36.4) 135 F.A. has / First instructions which will continue in charge of the Corps Main Depot will (When our Headquarters of 94th F.A. at U.24.c.2.0 (Sheet 27) the ADS at D.18.a.5.2 and forward posts and will be responsible for the evacuation of the front area - Move to be completed by 10 am 24 inst. MMM	
	22nd		Capt RAINEY RAMC with advanced party proceeded to ADS. D.18.a.5.2. 6 men taking over line. MMM	
	23rd		Remainder of personnel + equipment moved from Headquarters to ADS - Lieut TYREE	

WAR DIARY
INTELLIGENCE SUMMARY

Army Form C. 2118.

135th Field Ambulance
VOL 27 Page 3 —

Place	Date	Hour	Summary of Events and Information	Remarks and references to Appendices
A.D.S	1918 Aug 23rd		2nd Lieut STONER. R.A.R.C. proceeded attached to 94th F.A. from 136 & 137 F.A. remain at Quarry Wood and are attached to this unit — One (motor) Large Ambulance car attached for duty from 137 F.A. Relief of forward posts and A.D.S. completed at 12 noon — Information received from Royal Regt. (120th Inf Bde.) that two men to be returned as Brigade post — Quinton to commence at 4 p.m. Two motor ambulance cars = 36 stretcher bearers detailed from 136 F.A. as European reinforcement — Wounded started coming at 9.30. About 50 wounded passed thro' this A.D.S up to 1.30 a.m	
D18.a.5.2	24th		Headquarters of Ambulance moved from BLARINGHEM and took over Headquarters of 94th F.A at WALLON CAPEL U 24 c.2.0 — Maj W.R.P. McNEIGHT remained headquarters with Detachment from XV Corps Stm Cavls having handed over to a South African Field Ambulance.	
	25th		Maj McNEIGHT took over change of A.D.S. — 119 Inf Bde ordered to attack to march in	
	27th		27th Quinton to commence at 10 a.m	
		10.30 p.m	30 O.R. Shelton from unit on to TEXAS FARM to join holding party and be in readiness to proceed to A.D.S as reinforcement of regiment — Lieut Shelton and Hunloch sent to A.D.S — Bearer posts and relay posts reinforced	

Army Form C. 2118.

WAR DIARY
or
INTELLIGENCE SUMMARY
(Erase heading not required.)

135th Field Ambulance
VOL 27 Page 4

Place	Date	Hour	Summary of Events and Information	Remarks and references to Appendices
Headquarters	August 1918			
24.C.2.0 A.D.S.	27th	2 p.m.	Wounded arriving. 2 motor lorry ambulance cars brought up from 137"FA for evacuation	
D.18.a.6.2 Shunk	28th	midnight	Steady stream of wounded continues to come, mainly walking cases, evacuation satisfactory, no congestion	
36 A	28th		About 180 casualties passed through ADS up to 9 a.m. Bearers kept in touch with R.M.Os & Whip carried out.	
Headquarters D.9 d.1.8			Headquarters of Ambulance moved from WIELDON CHAPEL to TEXAS FARM D.9.d.1.8	
			A few wounded still being brought to A.D.S.	
	29th		At 1.30 p.m. 120th Bde (Major B--) pushed forward under a creeping barrage 11th Cameron Highlanders attacking – objective was taken with little opposition. Casualties are slight.	
	30th		40th Div RAMC order No 84 dated 30/8 issued 6 p.m. received to effect O.C. 137 FA will move forthwith to Church at Lt 17OTTE and open up a Main Dressing Station by 9 a.m. on 31st × × O C 135 FA will open forthwith an ADS at BRITANNIA FARM E 20 central & will move his headquarters to D 18 a 5-3. He will also reconnoitre and perform	

WAR DIARY
or
INTELLIGENCE SUMMARY.

135 Field Ambulance
Vol 27 Page 5

Army Form C. 2118.

Place	Date	Hour	Summary of Events and Information	Remarks and references to Appendices
	31st		an A.D.S. further formed - Maj J.R. BEVERIDGE D.A.M.C. arrived from Leer on 29th inst. on charge of A.D.S. & Lieuts from Maj McNEIGH who proceeded to England on one months Special leave - MMC Enemy reported returning along Dromond Front - Headquarters of Ambulance advanced to CANIEL CORNER. D.18.a.4.9 (old site of A.D.S.) A.D.S. which was moved to Bretanie Farm was advanced to E.24.a central in ruin of School House VIEUX BERQUIN - Enemy still retiring reported to be second east of DOULIEU - Ground east of A.D.S. reconnoitred in search of more advanced position for A.D.S. can note further forward as truck was prepared - owing to long range no of selling posts increased - new stretcher carriages made. Touch kept with R.A.M.C. Dags for Cucuation all due to shelling by enemy. No 71916 Pvt R H WATESON RAMC wounded by shell (GSW fracture femur - much rain during night rendering roads impassable for MMC. Lorry cars to a great extent.	

MM Monk Lieut Col RAMC
OC 135 F/A

Confidential

War Diary

of

135 Field Ambulance

from Sept 1/18 to Sept 30/18

(volume XXVIII)

A.J. Beveridge
Major RAMC
O.C. 135 Field Ambulance

Army Form C. 2118.

WAR DIARY
or
INTELLIGENCE SUMMARY.

(Erase heading not required.)

135 Field Ambulance.

Vol 28 - Page 1

Place	Date	Hour	Summary of Events and Information	Remarks and references to Appendices
Headquarters D.16.a.4.9. Sheet 36A	1918 Sept 1st		Advanced Dressing Station in ruined School house VIEUX BERQUIN. 119 B.M on battalion in front line advancing - Roads very bad after rain - Food Car and Horsed Ambulance went for found men - Reconnoitred found area for hunting for men ADS	MW
	"	7 p.m	A.D.S. moved on to CASEY FARM - 10 bunch shelter obtained from D.A.D.O.S for use at A.D.S.	MW
	2nd		Wounded other ranks from ADMS - 1/ post Div. Station CROIX DE BAC. - Been down - Motor cars & Morbid Stations to be obtained from 136 & 137 F.A. of regiment - 36 nurses taken out to BRITANNIA FARM -	
		12.30 a.m	Advanced Dressing Station moved forward to cutting at A.19. c.6.6. - Cars sent by hop cars to car reclining post on CASEY FARM. Them by Ford Car. "Front Ambulance Wagon" to Car post at Vieux Berquin - (owing to congestion of road) thence by large motor cars to M.D.S. COSLEY - (36A. E.21 a.9.4 - 137 F.A.)	MW
	3 p.m		Advanced Dressing Station moved forward to large farm at A.21. 6.2.8 - Nurses taken from BRITANNIA FARM moved on to CASEY FARM. -	
	3rd		BRITANNIA FARM named on to CASEY FARM - Standing in quietude about 60 casualties - wounded found through A.D.S	MW
	4th		No change - few casualties	MW

2353 Wt. W3544/1454 700,000 5/15 D. D. & L. A.D.S.S./Forms/C. 2118.

WAR DIARY
INTELLIGENCE SUMMARY

135th Field Ambulance

Vol 28 - Page 2

Army Form C. 2118.

Place	Date	Hour	Summary of Events and Information	Remarks and references to Appendices
Headquarters	1915 Sept			
D.18.a.4.9	5th		Advanced Dressing Station moved forward to A 24 d.2.1. - Farm been partly destroyed by enemy from and will be with annex and annexe as an A.D.S. - Bearer Post & Car Post at Verger Burgomen moved to site of A.D.S. at A 21 b.2.8. - 40 Div D.A.M.C. Order No 67 dated 6-9-18 received to effect - Main Dressing Station to be opened at 36A/F 30.c.4.6 (DONLIEU) by a portion of 136 F.A. by 12 noon on 6th inst - at 12 noon on 6th 137 F.A. will cease to function on M 9.8 & not become D.R.S. - x x x O.C. 137 will take over from O.C. 135 F.A. the H D S & all bearer posts and will be responsible for evacuation of all casualties for Div Front x x x O.C. 135 F.A. will take over Divisional Rest Station from 137 F.A. by 6 p.m. 8th inst. H.Q. 135 F.A. will move to Div Rest Station x x x Captn TROUNCE detached for temporary duty as M.O. Warwickshire Regt. (Reserve)	MW MW
	6th			
	7th		Preliminary arrangements for relief of 135 F.A. & forward area by 137 F.A. made -	

WAR DIARY
or
INTELLIGENCE SUMMARY.
(Erase heading not required.)

Army Form C. 2118.

135th Field Ambulance
Vol 28 - Page 3

Place	Date	Hour	Summary of Events and Information	Remarks and references to Appendices
Sheet 36 C/14.d.0.0 a.0.5 a.2.d.2.1	1915 Sept 8th	12 Noon	Handed over the evacuation of the whole of the Fauquissart Area to 137 Field Ambulance. 119th Brigade in the Line. Relief complete 12 noon. Capt Rainey, Lieut Caldwell and Lieut Qm Wood and 38 other ranks proceeded to Copley Cottage and took over the Divisional Rest station from 137 Field Amb	
Sheet 36A a.9000 Neuf Berquin E.2.1 a.94	8th	2 PM	Relief complete 2 PM. No of patients taken over 56. 119 Infantry Brigade order no 31 copy 1A received (Into Battalion relief in the Line) a/B	
	9th		Carried out improvements in buildings. A large amount of work in hand a/B	
	11th		Accommodation increased to 100. Two large store tents received from 136 Field Ambulance, one taken into use as a recreation tent for [...] days patients. The other to be used as a store tent. Dysentery very prevalent in the division. Weather cold wet wet. a/B	

Army Form C. 2118.

WAR DIARY
or
INTELLIGENCE SUMMARY.
(Erase heading not required.)

135th Field Ambulance
Vol 28 – Page 4

Place	Date	Hour	Summary of Events and Information	Remarks and references to Appendices
Sheet 36A 1/40,000 E.21.a.9.4.	12th		Capt Walker RAMC No 23 Clearing returned from leave. Lieut Phibbs RAMC rejoined Field Ambulance on relief by Capt Walker. Ops.	
	14th		Large Hospital kitchen completed also a billet for 27 men in COBLEY COTTAGE. Patients no 105 O/B	
	15th		Ten Sanitary Huts arrived under arrangements made by A.D.M.S.	
	17th		Lt Col O M Smith assumed command of F.A. on completion of temporary duty as acting A.D.M.S. 40 Div — 40th Division RAMC Order No 88 dated 17-9-18. Detail 17 7A relieved take over M.D.S. at F.29.6.6.9 from 136 F.A. on 18th inst x x x 136th F.A. will remain at LA BRIELLE FARM (2.5.a.6.0 approx) ready to move at 2 hours notice from Divisional Area —	
	20th		Lieut J L PHIBBS RAMC detached for temporary duty to 6th Royal Inns. Fusrs — Daily Statt – Remain 100 – Admitted 45 – to CCS 27 – to Duty 11 – Remain 106 – Diarrhoea - Remain 34 – Admitted 18 - to CCS 11 – to Duty 2 – Remain 39	
	22nd		Capt E W RAINEY detached for temporary duty with 13 Bn East Lancs. Continuing work at D.R.S. continued	

Army Form C. 2118.

WAR DIARY
or
INTELLIGENCE SUMMARY

135th Field Ambulance
Vol 25 - Pag. 5 -

(Erase heading not required.)

Place	Date	Hour	Summary of Events and Information	Remarks and references to Appendices
Hut 36.A.	1918 Sept 23rd		General routine at D.R.S. - Still a large number of sick & Diarrhoea cases Admits - Daily Total - Remaining - 101 - Admitted 30 to CCS 26 - to duty 3 - Remaining 101 - Admitting Divisional Pioneers	
21. a.9.4			Remaining 43 - 40 On Name Roll No 89. 23/8 received - not affecting the unit MDS (137¾A) to be closed at F 29 d 6.9 at 6 p.m. on 23rd inst. and opened at LA BRIELLE FARM (L.5 a 6.0) at same hour. MLC hand within Goods Kent Remaining 102 - Admitted 30 to CCS 13 - to duty 9 Remaining	
	26th		108 - Handed over command to Major O.J. Bennett MC - on returning to high/med on 14 days leave - S. M. Mack McPherson C.	
	27th		Information received that Lieut Colonel RN Stuart DSO has been appointed to command No 42 CCS	
		10.30 a.m.	Warry order received from A.D.M.S. 20 Division that Northern Corps heard army will attack at dawn 28th. In the event of an Enemy Retirement on the Corps front 137 will open a new A.D.S. in front of present A.D.S. and also a new M.D.S. 135 Field Amb will take over LA BRIELLE FARM as a Divisional Rest Station	

Army Form C. 2118.

135 Field Ambulance
Vol 28 Page 6

WAR DIARY
or
INTELLIGENCE SUMMARY.
(Erase heading not required.)

Instructions regarding War Diaries and Intelligence Summaries are contained in F. S. Regs., Part II and the Staff Manual respectively. Title pages will be prepared in manuscript.

Place	Date	Hour	Summary of Events and Information	Remarks and references to Appendices
Reek 36A 21.0.9.4.	29th		Weather very cold. No of patients one Officer 107 Other Ranks	A/3
	30th		Major W.R.P. McNaught Davies returned from special leave. Information received from A.D.M.S. 40 Division to effect that the 40 Division Boundary will extend northwards — the line reported 31.2 & 40 Division will run through 36/C.11 central to 36/C.16 central — Remains 1 Officer 102 O.R. — On Duty 9 — to C.C.S. 24 — Admitted 28	A/B

11/10/18

A J Beverley
Major RAMC
O.C. 135 Field Ambulance

Confidential.

War Diary

of

135 Field Ambulance

from 1st October 1918 to 31st October 1918.

(volume XXIX)

H Hardie
Lieut Col RAMC
O.C. 135th Field Ambulance

WAR DIARY or INTELLIGENCE SUMMARY

Army Form C. 2118.

135 Field Ambulance
Vol 29 Page 1

Place	Date	Hour	Summary of Events and Information	Remarks and references to Appendices
Sheet 36N 1918				
E.21.a.94	Oct 1st	10:15 AM	R.A.M.C. 9/B 40 Division R.A.M.C. Order no 91 Copy no 9 D/1/10/18 received. 137 Field Amb moved to Chateau in STEENWERCK and open Main Dressing Station. Ware by 4 P.m. Oct 2. 135 Field Ambulance move to LA BRIELLE FARM and open a Divisional Rest Station by 0900 hour Oct 3. Arranged details of relief with O.C. 137 Field Ambulance A/B	
	Oct 2	9.17 P.m.	Marched out from Cubby cottage leaving there a party of 2 Officers and 42 O.R. to take charge of 102 patients. Major W.R. McNaught R.A.M.C. in charge.	
36A/ a.6.0.	Oct 2	3:15 P.m.	Arrived at LA BRIELLE FARM and started work immediately on orders to open as a Divisional Rest Station on 8.h.3. Very large amount of constructional work in hand A/B	
	Oct 3	9 A.m.	Opened as a Divisional Rest Station. Received 18 patients before 6 P.m. Detachment and 93 patients moved to LA MOTTE CHATEAU. 36A/D.30.c.6.4. move completed at 4 P.m. A/B	

WAR DIARY or INTELLIGENCE SUMMARY

Army Form C. 2118.

135 Field Ambulance
Vol 29 Page 77

Place	Date	Hour	Summary of Events and Information	Remarks and references to Appendices
6A 5.a.6.0.	Oct 3	2 PM	Inspection by DDMS XV Corps. Verbal instructions received that Major W.R. McKnight RAMC is to proceed to XV Corps Headquarters as acting DADMS in our 6th for 14 days. G/B	
"	Oct 4	11 AM	Inspection by DMS II Army. Major General Lynn Moore AMS who expressed satisfaction at the work of the Divisional Rest Station. Party of 1 NCO and 10 men withdrawn from XV Corps Skin Centre at Le CINQ RUES (CHAZE BROUKE 54). 2 NCO's and 20 Bearers sent to 137 Field Ambulance G/B. Walter met our Col. Nich inreem Stamhone will president in Division. Daily State:- Admitted 1 Officer 25 OR. To CCS 1 Officer 12 OR. To Duty 7 OR Remain 125 OR D/5/10/18 Received G/S 40 Division RAMC order No 92 136 Field Ambulance to take over Main Dressing Plat at CHATEAU STEENWERCK. 137 Field Ambulance to move to LE HAYS FARM 36/B.28.d.7.8. on relief by 136 Field Ambulance. G/B	
6A 5.a.6.0	Oct 5th			

WAR DIARY or INTELLIGENCE SUMMARY.

Army Form C. 2118.

135 Field Ambulance
Vol 29 Page 111

Place	Date	Hour	Summary of Events and Information	Remarks and references to Appendices
L.5a.60 At BRIELLE FARM	1918 Oct 7		Weather cold and showery. 136 Field Ambulance relieved 40 Field Ambulance. Daily state:- Remains – 136 OR. To duty – 20 OR. To C.C.S. – 01 OR. Admitted – 37/0 OR 2 NCOs and 20 Bearers returned from 137 Field Ambulance a/s	
	1918 Oct 9th		Weather warmer. No of sick admitted increasing. Daily state. Remitted – 1 Officer – 31 OR. To C.C.S. – 17 OR. To duty 21 OR. Remains 1 Officer 129 Other Ranks. of which 1 Officer and 34 OR out at LA NISTE CHATEAU and the remainder at LA BRIELLE FARM a/s	
	1918 Oct 11		Inspection by the Divisional Commander who expressed his satisfaction on the running of the Divisional Rest Station a/s	
	1918 Oct 12		40th Division R.A.M.C. Order No 93 D/12/10/18. Copy as g received 137 Field Ambulance hand over the services of the Front	

WAR DIARY
or
INTELLIGENCE SUMMARY.

Army Form C. 2118.

135 Field Amb
Vol 29 Page IV

Place	Date	Hour	Summary of Events and Information	Remarks and references to Appendices
S.A.60.			On Oct 14th	
			line to 135 Field Ambulance and established a Divisional Rest Station at LE HAYS FARM. 136 continue to run the M.D.S. Preliminary arrangements made with 137 Field Ambulance Lieut Colonel R.N. Hunt D.S.O. returned from leave. A/B	
	13th		Lieut Carter R.A.M.C. proceeded to 13 East Lanc in relief of Capt Raine R.A.M.C. who returned to the unit. Weather cold and wet. A/B	
	14th	7AM	39 Bearer Sub offr Advanced Dressing Station at 36/H.4.C.5.4.	
		9AM	Capt Houseworth met Lieut Colwell with 10 demand depth to the slope of the advanced dressing Station	
		10AM	Lieut Colonel R.N. Hunt D.S.O proceeded to Front Army to take over command of 42 Casualty Clearing Station	
		1830	marched out with transport to new headquarter at 36/B.9.C.5.1. Arrive at 1530 men have good billets left	

Army Form C. 2118.

135 Field Ambulance
Vol 29 Page V

WAR DIARY or INTELLIGENCE SUMMARY.

Place	Date	Hour	Summary of Events and Information	Remarks and references to Appendices
B.9.C.81	14th		Capt Raines and 36 O.R. men at La Brielle Farm to take charge of that post till relieved by personnel of 137 Field Ambulance. Daily Stats — Admitted — 1 to C.C.S. To Duty — 1 Officer 14 Other Ranks remain 95 O.R. 40-8 main afternoon order no 218 received, Copy no 12	
B.9.C.81	15th		D 13/10/18 40-8 main is to attend in conjunction with Division on either side on the morning of the 15th Inspected the line and system of evacuation which is satisfactory. Major H. Harsh-Fpynmesides had assumed command of the Field Ambulance a/s	
	16th		Took over command from Major Beveridge with inspection next documents etc	98
	17th		A.D.S. moved to PERENCHIES 36/J.14. H.D. 9.20. to HOUPLINES 36/C.27. no battle casualties	188
	18th		A.D.S. moved to WAMBRECHIES 36/K.2. H.D. 9.25 to PERENCHIES & letter in the N of (arrived 16.30) to	

WAR DIARY or INTELLIGENCE SUMMARY.

Army Form C. 2118.

135/ FIELD AMBULANCE Vol. 29 page VI

Place	Date	Hour	Summary of Events and Information	Remarks and references to Appendices
36/K2.	19		WAMBRECHIES no battle casualties. Bridge over LA BASSÉE DEULE River destroyed but temporary bridge under construction by R.E. Bridge completed 06.00. A.D.S. moved a hundred pounded establishing in L'HOSPICE at CROIX. 136/K9. during the afternoon. A.D.S. an above establishment in a School. The building has been used for stables by the Germans, entailing a large amount of manual personnel cleaning up along some construction work.	14B
	20		H.D. War. seeing the sick of 120th & 138th BRIGADE. A.L.C. crew from tent 9 from A.D.S. evacuated to 137th F.A. Also at WAMBRECHIES	14A
36/K2	22		Still cleaning up - whitewashing etc. very little sick - a few civilians attending, no out patients. The division is now out of the line & is to undertake	14A 14A

135 F.A.
Vol. 29
page VII

Army Form C. 2118.

WAR DIARY
or
INTELLIGENCE SUMMARY.
(Erase heading not required.)

Place	Date	Hour	Summary of Events and Information	Remarks and references to Appendices
	23		road repairs. H.Q. and moved to CROIX to-day & joined with former A.D.S. Its functions were to form D.R.S. for 121st Brigade.	A¼
36/K	26	9.25	The division go into the line to-morrow & this F.A. is now to form D.R.S. for the whole division.	A¼
	28		H.Q. and moved to HOPITAL DE SECOURS RUE DE LA SAGESSE ROUBAIX & opened as a D.R.S. leaving 1 officer & about 20 O.R. behind to work the hospital at CROIX & also 1 officer + 2 O.R. to attend to civilian cases	A¼
	29		Rear party at CROIX joined H.Q. & Co. this morning bringing about 15 patients. During the afternoon chief of civilian cases were handed over to O.C. 8/8th F.A.	A¼

WAR DIARY
or
INTELLIGENCE SUMMARY.

135th Field Army Form C.2118
Vol. 29
page VIII

Place	Date	Hour	Summary of Events and Information	Remarks and references to Appendices
OUBAIX	31		Unit still functioning as a D.R.S. There are now 199 patients of whom 113 are influenza. This morning personnel were removed from the ANNEX to buildings outside the hospital & the ANNEX prepared for influenza patients. J Hornung Lt. Col. Comg 135th F.A.	A

135TH FIELD AMBULANCE.

No. ....
Date ....

WR 30
(40/3401)

COMMITTEE FOR THE
MEDICAL HISTORY OF THE WAR
Date 16 JAN 1919

Confidential

War Diary
of
135th Field Ambulance

from Nov 1/18 to Nov 30/18.

(volume XXX)

A. Hardin
Lieut Col
O.C. 135 Fd. Ambulance

WAR DIARY or INTELLIGENCE SUMMARY

138th Field Ambulance
Volume XXX
Page 1

Army Form C. 2118.

Place	Date	Hour	Summary of Events and Information	Remarks and references to Appendices
ROUBAIX	1/7/18	11	By taking over the ANNEXE dormitory to the nurses it has been arranged to increase to 260 & it can be still further increased by using the top floor. About 30 cases (influenza) further admitted to my including Major (Medical) R.A.M.C.	—
"	3/7/18		Daily state this morning showed 208 patients in hospital of whom 116 are influenza. The average number of influenza cases admitted daily exceeds the number to hospital staff. (only one receipt major Hospital staff) has contracted the disability. The result of Inspection this morning Patients in hospital this morning = 161. Influenza admissions dropped (Its 17 major. The result has been movement to C.C.S.	17/8
"	11/7/18		Capt. RAINEY & Capt. HAWKESWORTH rejoined	A2

WAR DIARY
or
INTELLIGENCE SUMMARY.

135th Field Amb Army Form C. 2118.
Vol. XXX
Page 11

Place	Date	Hour	Summary of Events and Information	Remarks and references to Appendices
ROUBAIX	11/11/18		Last night on completion of temporary duty with 13 Battalion. Major Benaressie in return entirely employed attending to the civil in sick. Lt BREAKEY is during the same 9/4 at ROUBAIX.	9/4
"	13/11		Patients in Hospital this morning 280 of return 122. There are influenza. Personnel arriving to-day from field ambt at U.S. 13 b. GAMBETTA to no. 147 in the Same 13 b.	14A
"	16/11		Personnel both R.A.M.C. & A.S.C. H.T. have been moved into billets in inhabited houses this day. They have complained very much of the coldness of their billets particularly a large empty Pharm. Surgeon pr 1NG & E. R.N. Evening 137 - F.A. Compt purged proceeded to R.I.R. for temporary duty.	

WAR DIARY 136th FIELD AMB Army Form C. 2118
INTELLIGENCE SUMMARY
Vol. XXX Page 111

Place	Date	Hour	Summary of Events and Information	Remarks and references to Appendices
ROUBAIX			No. of patients in hospital 16 9 O.R. up to date 938 have been admitted evacuation 15 o.c.s. & 366 dischargd to duty. Admissions for influenza getting very numerous 94 number fluctuating from 30 each morning 25 & an low as 12. Capt. RAINEY R.A.M.C. proceeded	94
"	21		on 14 days leave & one Lance Corporal T.H. Thirkle R.A.M.C. proceeded for a farewell inspection by Major General GUISE-MOORES C.M.G. D.M.S. 2nd ARMY on 15-the Division paraded for inspection & afterwards they marched passed. Lieut. E.P. NORWOOD U.S.M.C. departed to report	94
"	24		to A.D.M.S. 66- Division, 3 other ranks were sent to March infantry to turn out by the division & gentlemen of 66th Division thus thus Lt. I. H.M. CALDWELL returned off leave thus day	94

WAR DIARY or INTELLIGENCE SUMMARY

Army Form C. 2118.

135th F.A.
Vol. XXX
Page IV

Place	Date	Hour	Summary of Events and Information	Remarks and references to Appendices
ROUBAIX	24		Admissions for influenza are still high 33 yesterday May 17.11	
	29	8-6	Admissions for influenza yesterday 8.4 & on 25th 25. Evacuation is taking place at 11.00 & 14.00 daily.	
"	30		Admissions for influenza have dropped to-day, only 13 have come in. Since the 1st of the month 132 3 cases have been admitted to the F.A. of there 65 cases had influenza, 617 cases have been evacuated to C.C.S & 6th 7 returned to Unit. During the latter half of the month a Unit School of Instruction has been developed & is now in full swing. Two good rooms have been obtained for lecturing purposes & private Study & Classes are regularly held twice weekly in the following subjects: FRENCH,	A.R.

2353 Wt. W2544/1454 700,000 5/15 D.D.&L. A.D.S.S./Forms/C. 2118.

WAR DIARY or INTELLIGENCE SUMMARY

Army Form C. 2118.

135th F.A
Vol. XXX
page V

Place	Date	Hour	Summary of Events and Information	Remarks and references to Appendices
DUBAIX	30		BUILDING CONSTRUCTION CHEMISTRY, MATHEMATICS DRAWING & SHORTHAND. In addition N.C.O. and men are writing at their monthly under arrangements worked by the A.D.G.S. The personnel are now housed in private homes & are very comfortable. Trips by motor lorry are being arranged this week to visit places of interest. There are much amusements provided for students other amusements. 1/5 a weekly uniform once 4 personnel are by the division. to and a (3) contents.	

P. Hendin Lt. Col
R. Game
OKG 135 F.A.

WO 31
13464

21
Dec 1918

Confidential

War Diary
of
135 Field Ambulance

from 1st December, 1918 to 31st December, 1918.

(Volume 31)

COMMITTEE FOR THE
MEDICAL HISTORY OF THE WAR
Date 6 MAR 1919

139th FIELD AMBULANCE
Vol. XXXI
Page I

WAR DIARY
or
INTELLIGENCE SUMMARY.
(Erase heading not required.)

Place	Date	Hour	Summary of Events and Information	Remarks and references to Appendices
ROUBAIX	1/12/18		All 5 ton lorries are now gone to XVth Corps. Open centre run by 136 F.A. This gives 3 extra wards for general medical cases. The personnel to fill & staff nothing under high pressure. General orders have to-day been transferred to ANNEXE 4 WARDS 9 to 11 thence to influenza.	AH
"	6/12/18		Strength this day 4 medical by A.D.M.S. to 23rd CHESHIRE Regt. Capt. Pollock & Pierce 9 to 11 Hospital ready for use. The whole of 1st floor three important wards & the 2nd ward in the ANNEXE given up to influenza. Thirty-nine cases admitted yesterday.	AH
	7/12/18		Anti-influenza units — 119 Brigade, 135 & 137 F.A. & XV CORPS Cyclists Bn. — are collected in ward 6	AH

WAR DIARY
or
INTELLIGENCE SUMMARY.

13th FIELD AMB 13th wL Army Form C. 2118.

Vol. XXXI
Page II

Place	Date	Hour	Summary of Events and Information	Remarks and references to Appendices
ROUBAIX	12/10/18		Capt. PHIBBS R.A.M.C. reported for duty from the ROYAL I. RIFLES. Numbers in Hospital are about 160, numbers taken on duty (no out-patients) are between 50 & 60. We request of O.C. F.P. compound sent in officer to inspect the building & have an angle itto to send an officer this day at (17.00 hrs.) 18th	
"	13/12/18		Patients remaining this morning = 185. The first two Surrendered as Civilians left 11 12/15. The 2 entired Surgeon attached to no. 62 C.C.S. COURTRAI is now coming here for duty with the CORPS from monday & thursday each week. Work going on as general – Hospital full	
"	14/12/18		& now being carried from the dump on the canal bank to improve the hospital compound & wards.	

135th FIELD AMBULANCE
Vol. XXXI
Page III

WAR DIARY
or
INTELLIGENCE SUMMARY.

Place	Date	Hour	Summary of Events and Information	Remarks and references to Appendices
RUAIX	20/7/18		Work proceeding as usual. The numbers in hospital are falling off & the admissions for influenza are decidedly lower. Nothing out of the usual routine. Numbers remaining to-day is 144 including 4 officers.	A.N
"	24		Grateful to our Red Cross down over the whole of the hospital 8 prams.	A.A
"	26		Work returned to a minimum. Explicitly. The whole personnel with all "up" hutments had dinner together — about 260 set down; hutments was provided. In the evening there was a supper followed by a smoking concert from 9-11 pm	A.A
"	31		Work proceeding as usual. About 20 N.C.O. & men have proceeded to England under the terms of A.R.O v 2 Army no. 3429 d/22.12.16 & are not expected to return. In accordance with orders received A.A

130th FIELD AMBULANCE
VOL. XXXI
PAGE IV

WAR DIARY
or
INTELLIGENCE SUMMARY
(Erase heading not required.)

Army Form C. 2118.

Place	Date	Hour	Summary of Events and Information	Remarks and references to Appendices
DUDAIX	31		from D.G.M.S allowing units never have movements endorsed "To return to unit" as the full strength is necessary for running this D.R.S. The following is a summary of the work during the month of the unit during the month:- Admissions 974 Evacuations 686 Discharged to duty 444 Admissions for Influenza 420 Medical Inspection Room Number treated = 1697 P. Marchit Lt. Col. R.A.M.C O.C. 130th F.A.	

Confidential   40 DIV   WR 32
                Box 2418

War Diary
of

135 FIELD AMBULANCE.

from 1st January, 1919.   to 31st January, 1919

(VOLUME XXXII)

WAR DIARY or INTELLIGENCE SUMMARY

130th FIELD AMBULANCE
Vol. XXXII
Page 1
Army Form C. 2118.

Place	Date	Hour	Summary of Events and Information	Remarks and references to Appendices
ROUBAIX	6/1/19		Work proceeding as usual. Number in Hospital somewhat larger — 130 this morning. The T.F.G. before G.O.C visited the Unit this afternoon as a result of my application for him. He has moved certain recommendations which will be put in force forthwith. He recommended applying for Royal permission of another truck. entrance at Rue ste Fr.	
ROUBAIX	7/1/19		Lieut Colonel Harding R.A.M.C. proceeded on 14 days leave to England. Major A.J. Beverly R.A.M.C. assumed command of Unit. Capt. E.H. Rainy returned from leave 3/13	
"	8/1/19		Major W.R.P. McKnight proceeded on 14 days leave to England 3/13	
"	10/1/19		Demobilisation moving very fast 4 O.R. proceeded from unit to Army Concentration Camp at St ANDRE for demob.	

Army Form C. 2118.

WAR DIARY
or
INTELLIGENCE SUMMARY.
(Erase heading not required.)

Place	Date	Hour	Summary of Events and Information	Remarks and references to Appendices
ROUBAIX	10/1/19		To-day various trades o/s	
"	12/1/19		Nothing of general interest to report. Daily state Remains 1 Officer 128 other ranks admitted 18 O.Rs. to C.C.S. 11 O.Rs. to duty 9 O.R. 5 O.R ays to Corps Rest Camp	
"	15/1/19		Daily state remains 1 Officer 126 O.R. admitted 16 O.R. to C.C.S. 8 O.R. to duty 14 O.R. to 136 F.A (Corps Rest Camp) 2 O.R. Marked decline in Influenza. o/s	
"	20/1/19		Inspected by ADMS 40 Division who expressed satisfaction at the running of the hospital. Lieut Greer returned from leave and reported for 136 Field Ambulance. Lieut Brooks MORC placed on sick list o/s	
"	21/1/19		Weather cold but fine	

135.4 F.A
Vol. XXXII
Page 3

Place	Date	Hour	Summary of Events and Information	Remarks and references to Appendices
ROUBAIX	28		Work proceeding as usual. Numbers in hospital gradually falling & the work at the M.I. Room also lessening this morning's state 1 Officer & 56 O.R. remaining.	144
"	29		Weather hard - snow falling night 3 inches deep. Unit Strength 2 / 3 W.Os & Sergeants, now much Gros Guerre have not been under than R.administration and up since Jan. 12	144
"	31		Received verbal orders to my/from D.D.M.S. X Corps to evacuate by ambulance Piston & C.&H. M.C. by the hospital but limit by Feb "6th". This will out up all stretcher & ambulance at once the number of beds to about 60 by O.R. The ANNEXE was handed over to the ARMY Dental authorities on 29 & unit accommodated when for the dental surgeons	144

Army Form C. 2118.

WAR DIARY 10 & F.A. Vol. XXII
or
INTELLIGENCE SUMMARY. 10 apr 4

(Erase heading not required.)

Place	Date	Hour	Summary of Events and Information	Remarks and references to Appendices
OURAN	31		at 22 Rue du CHATEAU as it is impossible to recommence turn in the small front of building left to this unit. Found the strength to bring general more than required 8-11 a dozen to disappointment by the unit. Transferred 3 277 to O.B.S. 264 Lnty Smith interests 1427 comth TFA	M

M. Murphy Lt. Col.
Comdg. 130-F.A.

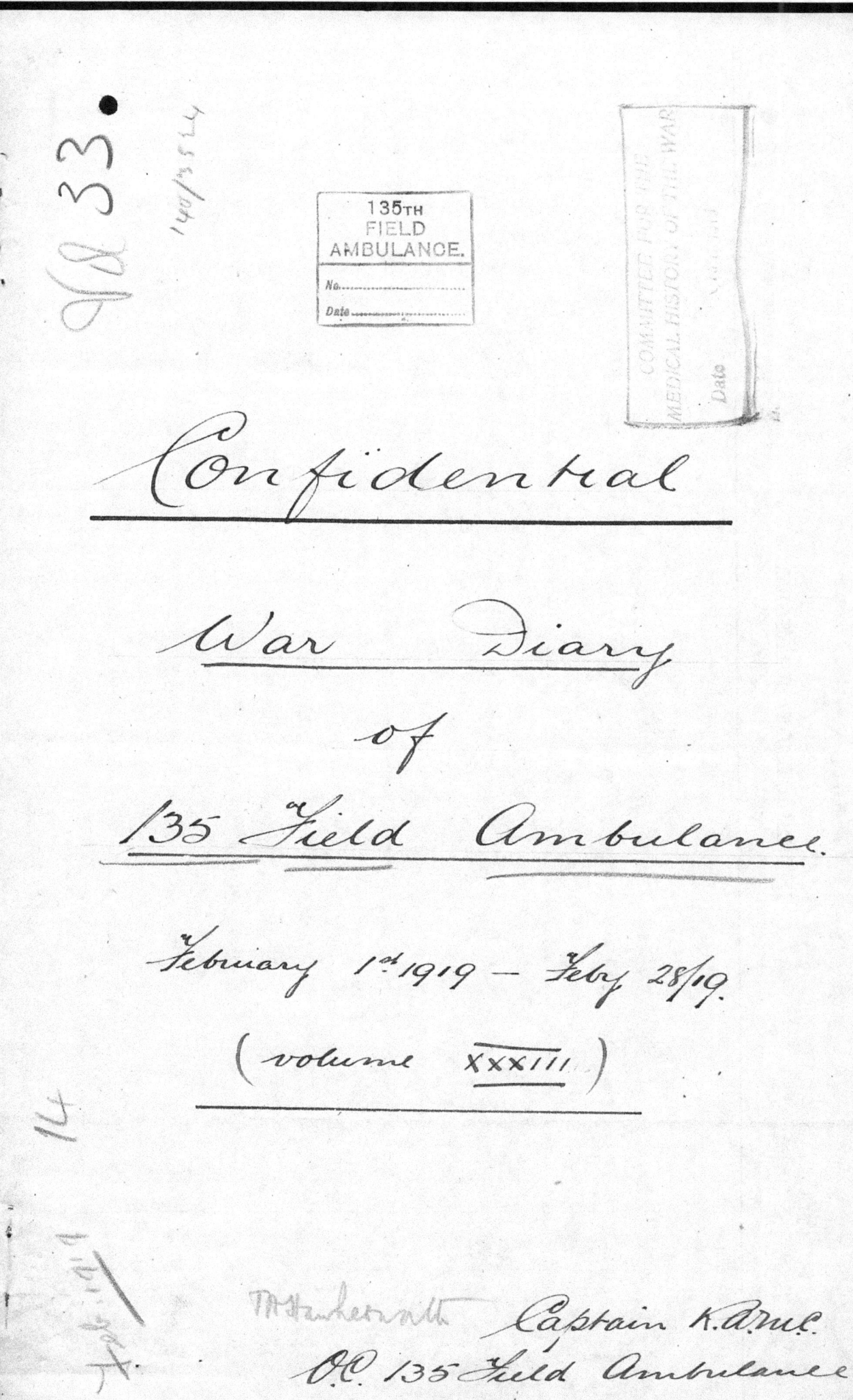

WAR DIARY or INTELLIGENCE SUMMARY

Army Form C. 2118.

133rd FIELD AMBULANCE
Vol. XXIII
Page I

Place	Date	Hour	Summary of Events and Information	Remarks and references to Appendices
ROUBAIX	4/2/19		During the last few days all spare men have been employed in cleaning the central block & Chapel ward. This is often practically complete & the men though the ten nurses in the new room to-day. Numbers in Hospital a.m.	144
"	9/2/19		Walls & O.C. ordered B lock & Chapel wing wing entirely re-enated & & ft. felt boards not been received by the French yet. Numbers in Hospital a.m.	172
"	16/2/19		Numbers in Hospital this morning 21 Major McNeight proceeded for demobilization on 14th a Major Burrudge M.C. is now acting D.A.D.M.S. Corps. & has been struck off strength of unit	198
"	23/2/19		No. in Hospital this morning 19. Work proceeding	

WAR DIARY
INTELLIGENCE SUMMARY.

Army Form C. 2118.

13ᵗʰ F.A.

Vol. XXX. III
page II

Place	Date	Hour	Summary of Events and Information	Remarks and references to Appendices
Rou 13AIT	23/2/19		normally. All equipment is being checked & collected togather in blocks according to F.S. manual	AA
"	1/3/19		The Patients remaining in Hospital were evacuated on the 25ᵗʰ at the Woodshed. Col Harding left for 14 days leave 26/2/19. Capt Haldeman taking over. Wyrroly to command of the Unit. The remaining Wing of the School building was packed over to the French authorities 28/2/19.	TRK

O.C. 13ᵗʰ S. Andrews
Lieutenant Colonel

Confidential

War Diary

of

135" Field Ambulance

March 1/19 to March 31/19

(volume XXXIV)

Capt. COL. R.A.M.C.
O.C. 135 FIELD AMBULANCE.

135th FIELD AMBULANCE
Vol XXXIV
Page 1

WAR DIARY
or
INTELLIGENCE SUMMARY.
(Erase heading not required.)

Army Form C. 2118.

Place	Date	Hour	Summary of Events and Information	Remarks and references to Appendices
Roobay	4/7/19		Capt B.H Raines and crew to Base from 11 CCS on 24/7/19 was struck off the strength accordingly. J.M.K	
"	7/19		Capt J Stuart Morin returned from belated comp. & proceeded to S.A.S.i Creolotin Camp A.D.S. J.M.K	
"	15/3/19		Capt J. Yeo Evac. to Hospital & struck off the Strength. J.M.K	
"	16/3/19		Lieut van der Hyden's Nobilisation. Unit now down to 6 officers & R.M.C. excepting 8 of A.S.C. coys & cheese & bear Otis despensed with service. Orders received from A.D.M.S to do for that that to be reduced even M.T. J.M.K	
"	17/7/19		Motor Reserve from 40 D Hop Yar to Carso settled unit to been reduced to [illegible] necessary since 4 Feb 19 J.M.K	
"	18/7/19		Capt H P B McCarter on 3rd attack off to strength for being demobilised, Act/Maj J Crawford M.C take a charge	
"			from 24/7/19 proceed to D.M.S 23 hrs first Feb. 19 J.M.K	
"	28/7/19		Lt Col H Irving returned from leave. J.M.K	
"	29/7/19		Lt Col Irving & Capt It G Butler D.S.M.C Response to Sheepl D.M.S St Area. J.M.K	
"	31/7/19		Lt Col Irving & relinquished command of Unit & proceed to D.M.S 2nd Army probs by Withdraw from D.M.S. J.M.K	

Wakeman
Capt R.A.M.C.

135TH FIELD AMBULANCE.
No.............
Date............

Confidential

War Diary
of
135 Field Ambulance
from Apl 1/19 to Apl 30/19.
(volume. XXXV)

U Hubernate
Capt Paul
135 Field Ambulance

Army Form C. 2118.

WAR DIARY
or
INTELLIGENCE SUMMARY.
(Erase heading not required.)

135th Field Ambulance
Volume XXXV. page I.

135TH FIELD AMBULANCE.

Instructions regarding War Diaries and Intelligence Summaries are contained in F. S. Regs., Part II. and the Staff Manual respectively. Title pages will be prepared in manuscript.

Place	Date	Hour	Summary of Events and Information	Remarks and references to Appendices
ROUBAIX	19/6/19		Lt/QM T. Wood DCM. proceeded on 14 days leave to UK	
	20/6/19		Capt HG Brooks MC USA proceeded to Cologne on 3 days leave	
	25/6/19		Capt HG Brooks MC USA proceeded to St Aignan, France, for demobilisation, under orders received from 9th HQ Areas Fx Force.	
			U Hazlenutt Capt RAMC	

Confidential

War Diary

of

135 Field Ambulance

from 1/5/19 to 31/5/19.

(volume XXXVI)

W Stalworth
Capt RAMC
O.C. 135 Field Ambulance

WAR DIARY
or
INTELLIGENCE SUMMARY.

Army Form C. 2118.

135 Field Ambulance
Volume XXVI

Place	Date	Hour	Summary of Events and Information	Remarks and references to Appendices
ROUBAIX	5/5/19		Lt & QM T. Wood DCM returned from leave	DOK
	12/5/19		Orders received from ADMS V/Area that this Unit is not to go home as Cadre but will be broken up in France	UH
	16/5/19		Orders received from HQ V Area (Q) that this unit is to form a Cadre & will be April 5. 19th	
	28/5/19		Notification received from H.Q. XV Corps that the Cadre Strength will be reduced by 75%, & the original Cadre Strength. No orders yet received for disposal of personnel these details	

Lt Col Koniath
Cof RAMC